Introduction

There is no better way to top off a wonderful meal
than with a delicious dessert. And even if your
meal is an ordinary one, the perfect dessert will
make it special. Easy Desserts Anyone Can Make
is filled with recipes for nearly 400 of those perfect
desserts. We're sure you'll find a dessert
to compliment every menu and occasion
and the simplicity of the recipes allows you
to create a special dessert with minimal time
and effort.

Desserts help make happy memories
and with this book, it's especially easy to
provide scrumptious desserts and all the
happiness that comes with them for your family.
Whether made specifically to honor a member
of the family, to celebrate an accomplishment or
just to add some joy to a regular day,
your family will love these desserts.

Table of Contents

Table of Contents

Pies
&
Cobblers

Strawberry-Cream Cheese Pie

2 (10 ounce) packages frozen,
   sweetened strawberries, thawed   2 (280 g)
2 (8 ounce) packages cream cheese, softened   2 (227 g)
⅔ cup powdered sugar   160 ml
1 (8 ounce) carton whipped topping   227 g
1 (9 inch) prepared chocolate crumb piecrust   23 cm

- Drain strawberries and reserve ¼ cup (60 ml) liquid.
- In mixing bowl, combine cream cheese, reserved liquid, strawberries and sugar and beat well.
- Fold in whipped topping and spoon into piecrust.
- Refrigerate overnight and garnish with fresh strawberries.

Strawberry Fluff Pie

32 marshmallows
½ cup milk   120 ml
¾ cup sliced strawberries, divided   180 ml
1 (8 ounce) carton frozen
   whipped topping, thawed   227 g
1 (9 inch) piecrust, baked   23 cm

- Combine marshmallows and milk in medium saucepan over medium heat. Cook and stir until marshmallows melt. Remove from heat and cool.
- Fold in ½ cup (120 ml) strawberries and frozen whipped topping. Pour into piecrust.
- Arrange remaining strawberry slices on top and chill before serving.

Cool Strawberry Pie

This recipe makes enough for two pies. The strawberry gelatin mixture is refreshing and not overly sweet. Freeze the extra one or give it away.

1 (16 ounce) bag frozen, unsweetened strawberries, thawed	.5 kg
1 (6 ounce) package dry strawberry gelatin mix	168 g
1 cup boiling water plus 1 cup cold water	240 ml
1½ cups whipping cream, divided	360 ml
2 (6 ounce) graham cracker piecrusts	2 (168 g)

+ Purée strawberries in blender or food processor.
+ Place gelatin in large bowl. Pour boiling water into gelatin and stir until gelatin dissolves.
+ Stir in cold water and strawberry purée. Chill until mixture thickens slightly, about 1 hour.
+ Beat whipping cream until peaks form. Chill until ready to serve.
+ Beat gelatin mixture on high speed for 2 minutes or until mixture is frothy. Fold in two-thirds of whipped cream and reserve one-third for garnish.
+ Spoon into piecrusts. Chill several hours until firm. Garnish with remaining whipped cream.

Snappy Strawberry Pie

This 5-minute, easy-to-make pie combines sweet and tart flavors. For a really great presentation, add some sliced kiwi to the top with strawberries. The bright colors really stand out and give it a festive look.

1 (14 ounce) can sweetened condensed milk	396 g
1 to 2 lemons	
4 ounces frozen whipped topping, thawed	114 g
1 (6 ounce) graham cracker piecrust	168 g
1 pint strawberries, hulled, halved	.5 kg

- Squeeze lemons to get ¼ cup (60 ml) lemon juice.
- In medium bowl, combine sweetened condensed milk with lemon juice and whisk until they blend well.
- Gently fold in whipped topping and pour mixture into prepared piecrust.
- Arrange strawberry halves in attractive design on top. Keep chilled until ready to serve.

Yum-Yum Strawberry Pie

2 pints fresh strawberries, divided	1 kg
1¼ cups sugar	300 ml
3 tablespoons cornstarch	45 ml
1 (9 inch) graham cracker piecrust	23 cm
1 (8 ounce) carton whipping cream, whipped	227 g

- Crush 1 pint (.5 kg) strawberries, add sugar, cornstarch and a dash of salt and cook on low heat until thick and clear. Cool.
- Place other pint of strawberries in piecrust and cover with cooked mixture.
- Top with whipped cream and refrigerate.

Strawberry-Yogurt Pie

1 (12 ounce) carton frozen whipped topping	340 g
1 (1 pint) carton strawberry yogurt	.5 kg
½ cup sliced strawberries	120 ml
1 (6 ounce) graham cracker piecrust	168 g

+ Combine whipped topping and yogurt and blend well.
+ Fold in strawberries.
+ Pour mixture into piecrust and freeze until firm.

Strawberry-Almond Pie

2 (10 ounce) packages frozen, sweetened strawberries, thawed	2 (280 g)
24 large marshmallows	
1 (8 ounce) carton whipped topping	227 g
¼ cup slivered almonds, chopped, toasted	60 ml
1 (9 inch) shortbread piecrust	23 cm

+ Drain strawberries but reserve juice.
+ In saucepan, heat strawberry juice and slowly add marshmallows. Heat on low and stir until marshmallows melt. Chill.
+ Fold in whipped topping and strawberries and pour into piecrust.
+ Sprinkle chopped almonds over top and refrigerate several hours.

Strawberry-Fruit Pizza

1 (18 ounce) package sugar cookie dough	510 ml
1 (8 ounce) package cream cheese, softened	227 g
½ cup sugar	120 ml
1 pint strawberries or raspberries	.5 kg
⅓ cup strawberry jelly	80 ml

- Preheat oven to 350° (176° C).
- Spread cookie dough onto ungreased pizza pan. Bake for 10 to 15 minutes or until dough is lightly browned around edges and cooked in middle.
- Remove from oven and cool.
- Blend cream cheese and sugar until light and fluffy. Spread mixture over cooled crust.
- Arrange strawberries on top. Warm strawberry jelly and brush over strawberries with pastry brush for glaze.
- Chill before serving.

Merry Berry Pie

1 (6 ounce) package strawberry gelatin mix	168 g
1 cup whole cranberry sauce	240 ml
½ cup cranberry juice cocktail	120 ml
1 (8 ounce) carton whipped topping	227 g
1 (9 inch) piecrust, baked	23 cm

- Dissolve gelatin in 1 cup (240 ml) boiling water. Add cranberry sauce and juice and chill until it begins to thicken.
- Fold in whipped topping, chill again until mixture mounds and pour into piecrust.
- Refrigerate several hours before serving.

Old-Fashioned Blueberry Pie

4 cups fresh blueberries	.9 L
¾ cup sugar	180 ml
¼ cup flour	60 ml
2 tablespoons lemon juice	30 ml
2 (9 inch) piecrusts, unbaked	2 (23 cm)
2 tablespoons (¼ stick) butter	30 ml

- Preheat oven to 425° (220° C).
- In large bowl, gently mix blueberries and sugar. (If blueberries are tart, add a little more sugar.) Stir in flour and lemon juice. Spoon mixture into pie pan over bottom crust.
- Dot with butter and place top crust over pie filling.
- Fold edges of top crust under edges of bottom crust to seal. Flute edges with fingers and cut several slits in top crust.
- Bake for 15 minutes and remove pie from oven. Cover edges of piecrust with foil to keep them from burning.
- Return to oven and bake for 30 to 40 minutes or until pie is bubbly and crust is golden brown.

Old-Fashioned Peach Pie

5 cups peeled, sliced fresh peaches	1.3 L
¾ cup sugar	180 ml
⅓ cup flour	80 ml
1 tablespoon lemon juice	15 ml
2 (9 inch) piecrusts, unbaked	2 (23 cm)
2 tablespoons (¼ stick) butter	30 ml

- Preheat oven to 425° (220° C).
- In large bowl, gently mix peaches and sugar. (If peaches are tart, add a little more sugar.) Stir in flour and lemon juice. Spoon mixture into pie pan over bottom crust.
- Dot with butter and place top crust over pie filling.
- Fold edges of top crust under edges of bottom crust to seal. Flute edges with fingers and cut several slits in top crust.
- Bake for 15 minutes and remove pie from oven. Cover edges of piecrust with foil to keep them from burning.
- Return to oven and bake for 15 to 20 minutes or until pie is bubbly and crust is light, golden brown.

Old-Fashioned Cherry Pie

4 cups pitted cherries	.9 L
1¼ cups sugar	300 ml
¼ cup flour	60 ml
¼ teaspoon cinnamon	1 ml
2 (9 inch) piecrusts, unbaked	2 (23 cm)
2 tablespoons (¼ stick) butter	30 ml

+ Preheat oven to 425° (220° C).
+ In large bowl, gently mix cherries and sugar. Stir in flour and lemon juice. Spoon mixture into pie pan over bottom crust.
+ Dot with butter and place top crust over pie filling.
+ Fold edges of top crust under edges of bottom crust to seal. Flute edges with fingers and cut several slits in top crust.
+ Bake for 15 minutes and remove pie from oven. Cover edges of piecrust with foil to keep them from burning.
+ Return to oven and bake for 20 to 25 minutes or until pie is bubbly and crust is golden brown.

Cherry-Pecan Pie

1 (14 ounce) can sweetened condensed milk	396 g
¼ cup lemon juice	60 ml
1 (8 ounce) carton whipped topping	227 g
1 cup chopped pecans	240 ml
1 (20 ounce) can cherry pie filling	569 ml
2 (9 inch) graham cracker piecrusts	2 (23 cm)

- ⁺ Combine condensed milk and lemon juice, stir well and fold in whipped topping.
- ⁺ Fold pecans and pie filling into mixture.
- ⁺ Spoon into piecrusts. Chill overnight.

Old-Fashioned Pecan Pie

This vintage recipe is more than 75 years old and was passed down through mothers and daughters.

3 eggs, beaten	
1 cup sugar	240 ml
1 cup white corn syrup	240 ml
1 cup pecan halves	240 ml
1 teaspoon vanilla extract	5 ml
1 (9 inch) piecrust, unbaked	23 cm

- ⁺ Preheat oven to 300° (148° C).
- ⁺ Beat eggs and sugar until lemon colored. Add corn syrup, pecans and vanilla and mix well.
- ⁺ Pour into unbaked piecrust. Bake for 1 hour or until center of pie is set.

Frances Parham

Pecan Tassies

Crust:

1 cup (2 sticks) butter, softened	240 ml
2 (3 ounce) packages cream cheese, softened	2 (84 g)
2 cups flour	480 ml

Filling:

3 eggs, slightly beaten	
¼ cup (½ stick) butter, melted	60 ml
2 cups packed brown sugar	480 ml
1 cup chopped pecans	240 ml

- Preheat oven to 375° (190° C).
- Beat together 1 cup (240 ml) butter and cream cheese until smooth. Stir in flour until well blended.
- Refrigerate at least 30 to 45 minutes.
- Divide dough into 24 equal pieces and flatten each into 3-inch (8 cm) round. Fit each dough round into 1 mini muffin cup. (Dough will extend slightly above each cup.)
- Combine all filling ingredients and spoon about 1 tablespoon (15 ml) filling into each cup.
- Bake for 20 minutes or until pastry is light brown and filling is set.

Thanksgiving Pie

1 (15 ounce) can pumpkin	425 g
1 cup sugar	240 ml
2 eggs, beaten	
1½ teaspoons pumpkin pie spice	7 ml
1 (12 ounce) can evaporated milk	340 g
1 (9 inch) piecrust, unbaked	1 (23 cm)

- Preheat oven to 425° (220° C).
- In bowl, combine pumpkin, sugar, eggs, pumpkin pie spice, evaporated milk and a dash of salt and mix well.
- Pour mixture into piecrust and bake 15 minutes.
- Lower heat to 325° (162° C) and continue baking another
  50 minutes or until knife inserted in center of pie comes out clean.

Creamy Pecan Pie

1½ cups light corn syrup	300 ml
1 (3 ounce) package instant vanilla pudding mix	84 g
3 eggs	
2½ tablespoons (⅓ stick) butter, melted	37 ml
2 cups pecan halves	480 ml
1 (9 inch) deep-dish piecrust, unbaked	23 cm

- Preheat oven to 325° (162° C).
- Combine corn syrup, pudding mix, eggs and butter, mix well and stir in pecans.
- Pour into piecrust. (Cover piecrust edges with strips of foil to prevent excessive browning.)
- Bake for 35 to 40 minutes or until center of pie sets.

Million Dollar Pie

24 round, buttery crackers, crumbled
1 cup chopped pecans   240 ml
4 egg whites (absolutely no yolks at all)
1 cup sugar   240 ml

+ Preheat oven to 350° (176° C).
+ In bowl, combine cracker crumbs with pecans.
+ In separate mixing bowl, beat egg whites until stiff and slowly add sugar while still mixing.
+ Gently fold crumbs and pecan mixture into egg whites and pour into pie pan.
+ Bake for 20 minutes and cool before serving.

Chess Pie

½ cup (1 stick) butter, softened   120 ml
2 cups sugar   480 ml
1 tablespoon cornstarch   15 ml
4 eggs
1 (9 inch) piecrust, unbaked   23 cm

+ Preheat oven to 325° (162° C).
+ Cream butter, sugar and cornstarch. Add eggs one at a time and beat well after each addition.
+ Pour mixture into piecrust. (Cover piecrust edges with strips of foil to prevent excessive browning.)
+ Bake for 45 minutes or until center sets.

Creamy Sparkle Pie

1 (8 ounce) package cream cheese, softened	227 g
½ cup sugar	120 ml
2 oranges	
1 (8 ounce) carton whipping cream, whipped	227 g
1 (9 inch) prepared graham cracker piecrust	23 cm

+ In mixing bowl, beat cream cheese and sugar until smooth.
+ Grate orange rind for 2 teaspoons (10 ml) zest and squeeze oranges to make ⅔ cup (160 ml) juice. Fold zest and juice into cream cheese mixture
+ Fold cream cheese mixture into whipped cream and spoon into piecrust.
+ Refrigerate at least 4 hours before serving.

Easy Pumpkin Pie

2 eggs	
1 (20 ounce) can pumpkin pie filling	567 g
1 (5 ounce) can evaporated milk	143 g
1 (9 inch) deep-dish piecrust, unbaked	23 cm

+ Beat eggs lightly in large bowl. Stir in pie filling and evaporated milk.
+ Pour mixture into piecrust.
+ Cover edges of piecrust with foil to prevent excessive browning.
+ Bake at 400° (204° C) for 15 minutes. Reduce temperature to 325° (162° C) and bake another 40 minutes or until knife inserted near center of pie comes out clean. Cool.

Frozen Pumpkin Pie

2 quarts vanilla ice cream, softened	1.9 L
1 (15 ounce) can pumpkin	425 g
2 teaspoons pumpkin pie spice	10 ml
1 cup English toffee bits	240 ml
1 (9 inch) prepared graham cracker piecrust	23 cm

+ In bowl, combine all ingredients and stir until they mix well.
+ Pour mixture into piecrust and freeze several hours before serving.
+ Serve with whipped topping.

Sweet Potato Pie

1 (15 ounce) can sweet potatoes, drained, mashed	425 g
3 eggs	
1 cup sugar	240 ml
1 tablespoon butter, melted	15 ml
1 (9 inch) piecrust, unbaked	

+ Preheat oven to 350° (220° C).
+ In large bowl combine sweet potatoes, eggs, sugar and butter. Beat until all ingredients blend well.
+ Pour into unbaked piecrust and bake until brown, about 1 hour.
+ If desired, remove pie from oven about 5 minutes early and top with ½ cup (120 ml) pecans and 1 cup (240 ml) miniature marshmallows. Return to oven until marshmallows are light brown.

Black Forest Pie

This is definitely a party dessert, but the family will insist it should be served on a regular basis.

4 (1 ounce) bars unsweetened baking chocolate	4 (28 g)
1 (14 ounce) can sweetened condensed milk	396 g
1 teaspoon almond extract	5 ml
1½ cups whipping cream, whipped	360 ml
1 (9 inch) piecrust	23 cm
1 (20 ounce) can cherry pie filling, chilled	567 g

- In saucepan over medium low heat, melt chocolate with sweetened condensed milk and stir well to mix.
- Remove from heat and stir in extract. (This mixture needs to cool.)
- When mixture is about room temperature, pour chocolate into whipped cream and fold gently until combined.
- Pour into piecrust.
- To serve, place heaping spoonful of cherry filling over each piece of pie.

Chocolate-Cream Cheese Pie

1 (8 ounce) package cream cheese, softened	227 g
¾ cup powdered sugar	180 ml
¼ cup cocoa	60 ml
1 (8 ounce) container whipped topping, thawed	227 g
1 (9 inch) prepared crumb piecrust	23 cm
½ cup chopped pecans	120 ml

+ Combine cream cheese, sugar and cocoa in mixing bowl and beat at medium speed until creamy.
+ Add whipped topping and fold until smooth.
+ Spread into piecrust, sprinkle pecans over top and refrigerate.

Cheesecake Pie

2 (8 ounce) packages cream cheese	2 (227 g)
3 eggs	
¾ cup plus 4 tablespoons sugar	180 ml; 60 ml
1½ teaspoons vanilla extract, divided	7 ml
1 (8 ounce) carton sour cream	227 g

+ In mixing bowl, combine cream cheese, eggs, ¾ cup (180 ml) sugar and ½ teaspoon (2 ml) vanilla. Beat for 5 minutes.
+ Pour into sprayed 9-inch (23 cm) pie pan.
+ Bake at 350° (176° C) for 25 minutes. Cool for 20 minutes.
+ Combine 4 tablespoons sugar (60 ml), 1 teaspoon vanilla (5 ml) and sour cream and pour over cooled cake. Bake another 10 minutes.
+ Chill at least 4 hours and serve with any flavor fruit topping.

Chocolate Ice Cream Pie

2 quarts chocolate ice cream, softened	1.8 kg
3 (7 ounce) bars white chocolate-cookie candy, chopped	3 (198 g)
½ cup chopped pecans	120 ml
½ cup fudge sauce, heated	120 ml
1 (9 inch) prepared chocolate cookie piecrust	23 cm

+ Place softened ice cream in large bowl, stir in chopped candy and pecans and mix well.
+ Spoon mixture into piecrust and freeze.
+ Let pie stand at room temperature about 10 minutes before slicing. Spoon heated fudge sauce over each slice of pie.

Frozen Chocolate Pie

1 (8 ounce) carton whipped topping, divided	227 g
1 (9 inch) prepared chocolate piecrust	23 cm
1¼ cups cold milk	300 ml
2 (3.9 ounce) packages instant chocolate pudding mix	2 (114 g)
1 cup white chocolate chips	240 ml

+ Spread half of whipped topping into piecrust and freeze 10 minutes.
+ Pour milk into bowl and add pudding mix. Beat with wire whisk about 2 minutes. (Mixture will be thick.)
+ Fold in remaining whipped topping and white chocolate chips. Quickly pour mixture into piecrust.
+ Freeze several hours before cutting to serve.

Cool Chocolate Pie

22 large marshmallows	
2 (8 ounce) milk chocolate	
candy bars with almonds	2 (227 g)
1 (8 ounce) carton whipped topping	227 g
½ cup chopped pecans	120 ml
1 (9 inch) prepared graham cracker piecrust	23 cm

+ In top of double boiler, melt marshmallows and chocolate bars.
+ Cool partially and fold in whipped topping and pecans.
+ Pour mixture into piecrust. Refrigerate several hours before serving.

Mint-Chocolate Pie

1 cup mint-chocolate chip ice cream, softened	240 ml
1 cup frozen whipped topping, thawed	240 ml
¾ cup crushed chocolate sandwich cookies	
with mint filling, divided	180 ml
1 (9 inch) prepared chocolate cookie piecrust	23 cm

+ Combine ice cream, whipped topping and ½ cup (120 ml) crushed cookies.
+ Place mixture in piecrust and sprinkle remaining cookie crumbs over top.
+ Refrigerate 6 to 8 hours or until firm.

Chocolate-Coconut Pie

1½ cups flaked coconut	360 ml
1½ cups chopped pecans	360 ml
1 (12 ounce) package chocolate chips	340 g
1 (6 ounce) prepared graham cracker piecrust	
1 (14 ounce) can sweetened condensed milk	

+ Preheat oven to 350° (176° C).
+ Combine coconut, pecans and chocolate chips. Sprinkle mixture over piecrust.
+ Spoon sweetened condensed milk evenly over coconut mixture.
+ Bake for 25 to 30 minutes. Cool before serving.

Chocolate-Amaretto Pie

2 (7 ounce) milk chocolate candy bars with almonds	2 (198 g)
⅓ cup amaretto liqueur	80 ml
2 (8 ounce) cartons whipping cream, whipped	2 (227 g)
1 (9 inch) prepared shortbread piecrust	23 cm

+ Melt chocolate in double boiler over low heat. Remove from heat and pour in amaretto.
+ Stir chocolate and amaretto for 10 to 15 minutes until mixture cools to room temperature.
+ Fold in whipped cream.
+ Pour mixture into piecrust. Chill several hours before serving.

Solo Chocolate Pies

1 (3 ounce) package cook-and-serve vanilla pudding mix	84 g
1 cup plus ¼ cup miniature semi-sweet chocolate chips, divided	240 ml; 60 ml
1 (4 ounce, 6 count) package prepared miniature graham cracker piecrusts	114 g
Whipped topping	

+ Prepare pudding mix according to package directions. Remove from heat.
+ Immediately add 1 cup (240 ml) chocolate chips and stir until chips melt.
+ Set aside to cool, about 5 minutes, and stir occasionally.
+ Pour pie filling into individual crusts and cover with plastic wrap. Chill several hours until firm.
+ When ready to serve, place dollop of whipped cream on each individual pie and sprinkle with remaining ¼ cup (60 ml) chocolate chips.

Chilled Chocolate-Mocha Pie

2 tablespoons (¼ stick) butter	30 ml
1 (12 ounce) package semi-sweet or milk chocolate chips	340 g
2½ cups crispy rice cereal	600 ml
1 quart coffee ice cream, softened	1 L
3½ to 4 ounces shaved chocolate	114 g

+ Melt butter and chocolate chips in top of double boiler, set over simmering water and stir until mixture is smooth.
+ Remove from heat and stir in rice cereal.
+ Spread mixture evenly in bottom of 9-inch (23 cm) pie pan and chill until set.
+ Spread ice cream over chocolate-cereal crust and freeze for several hours.
+ Remove from freezer and garnish with shaved chocolate. Let pie sit at room temperature for a few minutes before serving.

Frozen Mud Pie

1 pint chocolate ice cream, softened	.5 kg
1 teaspoon instant coffee granules	5 ml
½ cup powdered sugar	120 ml
1 (8 ounce) carton whipping cream, whipped	227 g
1 (9 inch) prepared chocolate piecrust	23 cm

+ Place softened ice cream in mixing bowl and stir in coffee granules.
+ Stir powdered sugar into whipped cream and quickly fold into ice cream mixture.
+ Spoon into piecrust and freeze.

Coffee-Mallow Pie

1 tablespoon instant coffee granules	15 ml
4 cups miniature marshmallows	.9 L
1 tablespoon butter	15 ml
1 (8 ounce) carton whipping cream, whipped	227 g
1 (9 inch) prepared graham cracker piecrust	23 cm
½ cup chopped walnuts, toasted	120 ml

- In heavy saucepan, bring 1 cup (240 ml) water to boil and stir in coffee until it dissolves.
- Reduce heat and add marshmallows and butter. Cook and stir over low heat until marshmallows melt and mixture is smooth.
- Set saucepan in ice and whisk mixture constantly until it cools.
- Fold in whipped cream and spoon into piecrust. Sprinkle with walnuts.
- Refrigerate for at least 4 hours before serving.

Tumbleweed Pie

½ gallon vanilla ice cream, softened	1.9 L
⅓ cup plus 1 tablespoon kahlua	80 ml
⅓ cup plus 1 tablespoon amaretto liqueur	80 ml
1 (9 inch) prepared chocolate cookie piecrust	23 cm
¼ cup slivered almonds, toasted	60 ml

- Place ice cream, kahlua and amaretto in mixing bowl and blend as quickly as possible.
- Pour mixture into piecrust.
- Sprinkle almonds over top and freeze.

Grasshopper Pie

22 large marshmallows
⅓ cup crème de menthe   80 ml
1 (12 ounce) carton whipping cream, whipped   340 g
1 (9 inch) prepared chocolate piecrust   23 cm

+ In large saucepan, melt marshmallows with crème de menthe over low heat and cool.
+ Fold whipped cream into marshmallow mixture.
+ Pour filling into piecrust and freeze until ready to serve.

Piña Colada Pie

2 pints vanilla ice cream, softened   1.5 ml
1 (15 ounce) can crushed pineapple, drained   425 ml
½ cup flaked coconut   120 ml
2 tablespoons light rum   30 ml
1 (9 inch) prepared graham cracker piecrust   23 cm

+ Place ice cream in large bowl, stir in pineapple, coconut and rum and mix well.
+ Spoon into piecrust and freeze.
+ Remove pie from freezer about 10 minutes before slicing.

Tip: You can soften ice cream by placing it in the refrigerator for about 30 minutes.

Irish Cream Delight

½ cup milk	120 ml
32 large marshmallows	
⅓ cup Irish cream liqueur	80 ml
1½ cups whipping cream	360 ml
1 (6 ounce) chocolate cookie piecrust	168 g

+ Place milk and marshmallows in large saucepan over low heat. Stir constantly until marshmallows melt.
+ Remove mixture from pan and chill about 30 minutes, stirring occasionally. Mixture is ready if it mounds slightly when dropped from spoon.
+ Slowly add liqueur to marshmallow mixture and stir well after each addition.
+ While mixture is chilling, beat whipping cream in medium bowl until stiff peaks form. Cover and chill.
+ Gently fold marshmallow mixture into cream. Pour into piecrust. Cover and chill 3 to 4 hours until pie sets.

Holiday Pie

1 (8 ounce) package cream cheese, softened	227 g
1 (14 ounce) can sweetened condensed milk	396 g
1 (3.4 ounce) box instant vanilla pudding mix	100 g
1½ cups frozen whipped topping, thawed	360 ml
1 (9 inch) prepared graham cracker piecrust	23 cm
Holiday candies	

+ With mixer, beat cream cheese until smooth, gradually add condensed milk and beat well.
+ Add pudding mix and ¾ cup (180 ml) water, beat until smooth and fold in whipped topping.
+ Pour filling into piecrust and sprinkle with crumbled holiday candies.

Dixie Pie

24 large marshmallows	
1 cup evaporated milk	240 ml
1 (8 ounce) carton whipping cream, whipped	227 g
3 tablespoons bourbon	45 ml
1 (9 inch) chocolate piecrust	23 cm

+ In saucepan on low heat, melt marshmallows in milk and stir constantly. Do not boil.
+ Cool in refrigerator.
+ Fold marshmallow mixture into whipping cream while adding bourbon.
+ Pour into piecrust. Refrigerate at least 5 hours before serving.

Frozen Kahlua Pie

1 pint whipping cream	.5 kg
⅓ cup kahlua	80 ml
5 (1.4 ounce) chocolate-covered toffee candy bars, crushed	5 (43 g)
1 quart vanilla ice cream, softened	1 L
2 (9 inch) chocolate piecrusts	2 (23 cm)

+ With mixer, combine whipping cream and kahlua and beat until stiff peaks form.
+ Gently stir in toffee crumbs.
+ Fold in ice cream and mix well.
+ Spoon into piecrusts and freeze.
+ Remove from freezer about 10 minutes before slicing. If you like, garnish with chocolate shavings or crumbs from crushed chocolate cookies.

Toffee-Caramel Pie

2 (14 ounce) cans sweetened condensed milk	2 (396 g)
1 (6 ounce) graham cracker piecrust	168 g
1 pint whipping cream	480 ml
½ cup firmly packed brown sugar	120 ml
1 (1.4 ounce) chocolate-covered toffee candy bar, crushed	45 g

+ Preheat oven to 425° (220° C).
+ Pour sweetened condensed milk into 7 x 11-inch (18 x 28 cm) baking dish and cover with aluminum foil.
+ Create water bath by placing baking dish inside 9 x 13-inch (23 x 33 cm) baking dish and add enough hot water to the larger dish to come up the sides 1 inch (2.5 cm).
+ Bake for 1 hour 20 minutes until condensed milk is caramel colored and thick. If needed, add water to large baking dish during baking as it evaporates.
+ Remove smaller dish from larger dish, pour caramelized milk into prepared crust and cool.
+ Combine whipping cream and brown sugar in small bowl and beat until soft peaks form. Spread whipped cream over caramel filling and sprinkle crushed toffee over top.

Creamy Butterscotch Pie

1 (8 ounce) package cream cheese, softened	227 g
1 (14 ounce) can sweetened condensed milk	396 g
1 (3.4 ounce) package instant butterscotch pudding mix	98 g
1 (8 ounce) carton whipped topping, divided	227 g
1 (9 inch) graham cracker piecrust	23 cm

- In mixing bowl, beat cream cheese until creamy. Add condensed milk and mix well.
- On low speed, add pudding mix and ¾ cup (180 ml) cold water and beat until smooth.
- Fold in half of whipped topping and spoon mixture into piecrust.
- Refrigerate several hours before serving. Top each slice with remaining whipped topping.

Creamy Peanut Butter Pie

1 (8 ounce) package cream cheese, softened	227 g
1 cup sugar	240 ml
1 cup creamy peanut butter	240 ml
1 teaspoon vanilla extract	5 ml
1 (8 ounce) carton whipping cream, whipped	227 ml
1 (9 inch) prepared graham cracker piecrust	23 cm

- In mixing bowl, combine cream cheese, sugar, peanut butter and vanilla and beat until creamy.
- Fold in whipped cream and spoon mixture into piecrust and refrigerate.

Peanut Butter Pie

⅔ cup crunchy peanut butter	160 ml
1 (8 ounce) package cream cheese, softened	227 g
½ cup milk	120 ml
1 cup powdered sugar	240 ml
1 (9 inch) graham cracker piecrust	1 (23 cm)
1 (8 ounce) carton whipped topping	227 g

+ With mixer, blend peanut butter, cream cheese, milk and powdered sugar and fold in whipped topping.
+ Pour into piecrust. Refrigerate several hours before serving.

Banana-Cream Cheese Pie

1 (8 ounce) package cream cheese, softened	227 g
1 (14 ounce) can sweetened condensed milk	396 g
⅓ cup fresh lemon juice	80 ml
4 bananas	
1 (9 inch) chocolate piecrust	23 cm

+ In large bowl, beat cream cheese until light and fluffy. Gradually beat in sweetened condensed milk until mixture is smooth.
+ Slice bananas and dip slices in lemon juice. Drain and use half of slices to line crust. Reserve other half for topping.
+ Stir remaining lemon juice into cream cheese mixture. Pour filling over bananas. Arrange remaining banana slices on top of filling.
+ Cover and chill for several hours to set.

Banana-Vanilla Pie

1 banana, sliced	
1 (9 inch) prepared graham cracker piecrust	23 cm
2 cups cold milk	480 ml
⅓ cup sugar	80 ml
2 (3.4 ounce) packages instant	
vanilla pudding mix	2 (100 g)
1 (8 ounce) carton French vanilla	
whipped topping, divided	227 g

+ Place banana slices in piecrust.
+ Pour milk into medium bowl, add sugar and pudding mix and beat about 2 minutes. (Mixture will be thick.)
+ Fold in half of whipped topping and spoon mixture into piecrust.
+ Refrigerate several hours before serving. Top each serving with dollops of remaining whipped topping.

Banana Split Pie

3 small bananas	
1 (9 inch) prepared graham cracker piecrust	23 cm
1 quart vanilla ice cream, softened	1 L
Fudge sauce	
Whipped topping	
Chopped pecans	
Maraschino cherries	

+ Slice bananas and place on piecrust.
+ Spoon softened ice cream over bananas and freeze for 2 to 3 hours.
+ Pour fudge sauce over ice cream and top with a layer of whipped topping sprinkle with chopped pecans and place a cherry on top.

Peach-Mousse Pie

1 (16 ounce) package frozen peach slices, thawed	.5 kg
1 cup sugar	240 ml
1 (.25 ounce) packet unflavored gelatin mix	7 g
⅛ teaspoon ground nutmeg	.5 ml
¾ (8 ounce) carton whipped topping	¾ (227 g)
1 (9 inch) graham cracker piecrust	23 cm

- Place peaches in blender and process until smooth.
- Transfer peaches to saucepan, bring to boil and stir constantly.
- Combine sugar, gelatin and nutmeg and stir into hot purée until sugar and gelatin dissolve.
- Pour gelatin-peach mixture into large mixing bowl.
- Place in freezer until mixture mounds (about 20 minutes) and stir occasionally
- Beat mixture at high speed until it becomes light and frothy, about 5 minutes.
- Fold in whipped topping and spoon into piecrust.

Apricot Pie

2 (15 ounce) cans apricot halves, drained	2 (425 g)
1 (9 inch) piecrust, unbaked	23 cm
1¼ cups sugar	300 ml
¼ cup flour	60 ml
1 (8 ounce) carton whipping cream	227 g

- Cut each piece of apricot in half and arrange evenly in piecrust.
- Combine sugar and flour and sprinkle over apricots.
- Pour whipping cream over pie.
- Place foil over edges of piecrust to prevent excessive browning.
- Bake at 325° (162° C) for 1 hour 20 minutes.

Pineapple-Cheese Pie

1 (14 ounce) can sweetened condensed milk	396 g
¼ cup lemon juice	60 ml
1 (8 ounce) package cream cheese, softened	227 g
1 (15 ounce) can crushed pineapple, well drained	425 g
1 (9 inch) graham cracker piecrust	23 cm

- In mixing bowl, combine condensed milk, lemon juice and cream cheese.
- Beat slowly at first then beat until smooth. Fold in well drained pineapple and mix well.
- Pour into piecrust and chill 8 hours before slicing.

Pineapple Fluff Pie

1 (20 ounce) can crushed pineapple with juice	567 g
1 (3.4 ounce) package instant lemon pudding mix	100 g
1 (8 ounce) carton whipped topping	227 g
1 (9 inch) graham cracker piecrust	23 cm

- In mixing bowl, combine pineapple and pudding mix and beat until thick.
- Fold in whipped topping and spoon into piecrust.
- Chill for several hours before serving.

Pineapple-Lemon Pie

Eat one and freeze the other!

1 (14 ounce) can sweetened condensed milk	396 g
1 (20 ounce) can lemon pie filling	567 g
1 (20 ounce) can crushed pineapple, well drained	567 g
1 (8 ounce) carton whipped topping	227 g
2 (9 inch) cookie-flavored piecrusts	2 (23 cm)

+ With mixer, combine condensed milk and lemon pie filling and beat until smooth.
+ Gently fold pineapple and whipped topping into condensed milk mixture.
+ Pour into 2 piecrusts and refrigerate.

Sunny Lime Pie

Nothing could be easier!

2 (6 ounce) cartons key lime pie yogurt	2 (168 g)
1 (3 ounce) package lime gelatin mix	84 g
1 (8 ounce) carton whipped topping	227 g
1 (9 inch) graham cracker piecrust	23 cm

+ In bowl, combine yogurt and lime gelatin mix and blend well.
+ Fold in whipped topping.
+ Spread in piecrust and freeze. Take out of freezer 20 minutes before slicing.

Easy, Breezy Lemonade Pie

1 (6 ounce) can frozen lemonade concentrate, thawed	168 g
1 quart vanilla ice cream, softened	1 L
1 (8 ounce) can crushed pineapple, drained	227 g
1 (8 ounce) container whipped topping	227 g
2 (6 ounce) prepared graham cracker piecrusts	2 (168 g)

- Mix lemonade concentrate, ice cream and pineapple until they blend well.
- Fold in whipped topping and pour into prepared piecrusts.
- Freeze at least 4 hours before serving.

Optional: Garnish with lemon slices.

Creamy Lemon Pie

1 (8 ounce) package cream cheese, softened	227 g
1 (14 ounce) can sweetened condensed milk	396 g
¼ cup lemon juice	60 ml
1 (20 ounce) can lemon pie filling	567 g
1 (9 inch) graham cracker piecrust	23 cm

- In mixing bowl, beat cream cheese until creamy.
- Add sweetened condensed milk and lemon juice and beat until mixture is very creamy.
- Fold in lemon pie filling, stir until creamy and pour into piecrust.
- Refrigerate several hours before slicing and serving.

Mrs. Smith's Dressed-Up Apple Pie

1 (3 pound) frozen Mrs. Smith's Deep-Dish Apple Pie, thawed	1.3 kg

Praline Topping:

¼ cup (½ stick) butter	60 ml
1¼ cups packed brown sugar	300 ml
⅓ cup whipping cream	80 ml
1 cup powdered sugar	240 ml

+ Preheat oven to 375° (190° C).
+ Remove plastic wrap from pie, cut 4 or 5 slits in top of crust and place on baking sheet.
+ Bake 1 hour 20 minutes and shield top of pie with foil after 1 hour. Cool several hours.
+ In saucepan, combine butter, brown sugar and whipping cream. Bring to boil over medium heat and boil for 1 minute.
+ Remove from heat and stir in powdered sugar until mixture is smooth.
+ Slowly pour praline mixture over pie and spread to cover. If you like, sprinkle 1 cup (240 ml) chopped pecans over top.

Easy Graham Cracker Crust

24 graham cracker squares, crushed
⅓ cup (⅔ stick) butter, melted   80 ml
3 tablespoons sugar   45 ml

+ Preheat oven to 350° (176° C).
+ Mix graham cracker crumbs with butter and sugar.
+ Press mixture into 9-inch pie pan so bottom and side
  have same thickness.
+ Bake 5 to 10 minutes until crust is light brown. Cool
  before filling.

Cream Cheese Crust

½ cup (1 stick) butter, softened   120 ml
1 (3 ounce) package cream cheese, softened   84 g
1 cup flour   240 ml

+ Combine all ingredients and blend with fork or pastry
  blender until mixture holds its shape.
+ Form dough into ball and chill for about 1 hour.
+ Roll dough out onto floured surface.
  Yield: 1 (9 inch/23 cm) piecrust.

Apple Dumplings

1½ cups firmly packed brown sugar, divided	360 ml
¼ cup chopped pecans	60 ml
2 tablespoons (¼ stick) butter, softened	30 ml
6 baking apples, cored	
2 (9 inch) pastry shells	2 (23 cm)
½ cup water	120

+ Preheat oven to 425° (220° C).
+ Mix ½ cup (120 ml) packed brown sugar, pecans and butter in bowl and spoon mixture into each apple.
+ Roll pastry shells to ⅛-inch (.3 cm) thickness. Cut into 6 squares approximately 7 inches (18 cm) each .
+ Wrap 1 pastry square around each apple and pinch edges to seal.
+ Place remaining 1 cup (240 ml) packed brown sugar and water in saucepan over medium heat and stir until sugar dissolves. Pour syrup over dumplings.
+ Bake for 35 to 40 minutes or until tender and baste occasionally with syrup.

For even more flavorful dumplings, add 2 teaspoons (10 ml) cinnamon or apple pie spice along with sugar, pecans and butter.

Apple Crescents

1 (8 ounce) can refrigerated crescent rolls	227 g
2 Granny Smith apples, peeled, quartered	
1 cup orange juice	240 ml
1 cup sugar	240 ml
½ cup (1 stick) butter	120 ml
1 teaspoon cinnamon	5 ml

- Preheat oven to 350° (176° C).
- Unroll crescent dough and separate. Wrap each apple quarter with crescent dough.
- Place apple crescents in greased 9 x 13-inch (23 x 33 cm) baking dish.
- In saucepan, combine orange juice, sugar, butter and cinnamon and bring to boil. Pour orange juice mixture over crescents.
- Bake for 30 minutes or until golden brown and bubbly.

Apricot Cobbler

So easy and so good!

1 (20 ounce) can apricot pie filling	567 g
1 (20 ounce) can crushed pineapple with juice	567 g
1 cup chopped pecans	240 ml
1 (18 ounce) box yellow cake mix	510 g
1 cup (2 sticks) butter, melted	240 ml

- Preheat oven to 375° (190° C).
- Spray 9 x 13-inch (23 x 33 cm) baking dish with non-stick spray, pour pie filling in pan and spread.
- Spoon pineapple and juice over pie filling and sprinkle pecans over pineapple.
- Sprinkle cake mix over pecans.
- Drizzle melted butter over cake mix and bake for 40 minutes or until light brown and crunchy.
- Serve hot or room temperature. (It's great topped with whipped topping.)

Cherry-Strawberry Cobbler

1 (20 ounce) can strawberry pie filling	567 g
1 (20 ounce) can cherry pie filling	567 g
1 (18 ounce) box white cake mix	510 g
1 cup (2 sticks) butter, melted	240 ml
¾ cup slivered almonds	180 ml
Whipped topping	

- Spread pie fillings in greased 9 x 13-inch (23 x 33 cm) baking pan.
- Sprinkle cake mix over pie fillings, drizzle butter over top and sprinkle with almonds.
- Bake at 350° (176° C) for 55 minutes.
- Serve with dollops of whipped topping.

Double-Berry Cobbler

1 (12 ounce) package frozen raspberries	340 g
1 (12 ounce) package frozen blackberries	340 g
⅓ cup sugar	80 ml
⅓ cup flour	80 ml
¼ cup (½ stick) butter, melted	60 ml
½ (15 ounce) package refrigerated piecrust	½ (425 g)

- Preheat oven to 375° (190° C).
- In large bowl, combine raspberries, blackberries, sugar, flour and butter and mix well.
- Spoon berry mixture into greased 9 x 13-inch (23 x 33 cm) baking dish.
- Roll 1 piecrust to fit on top of berry mixture and sprinkle with extra sugar.
- Bake 1 hour or until golden brown and bubbly.

Blueberry Hill Crunch

1 (20 ounce) can crushed pineapple with juice	567 g
1 (18 ounce) box yellow cake mix	510 g
3 cups fresh or frozen blueberries	710 ml
⅔ cup sugar	160 ml
½ cup (1 stick) butter, melted	120 ml

- Spread pineapple in buttered or sprayed 9 x 13-inch (23 x 33 cm) baking dish.
- Sprinkle with cake mix, blueberries and sugar. Drizzle with butter. (If you really want to make it good, add 1 cup/240 ml chopped pecans.)
- Bake at 350° (176° C) for 45 minutes or until bubbly.

Express Fruit Cobbler

*Use any kind of fruit pie filling to create this fast,
last-minute cobbler for a great dessert.*

2 (20 ounce) cans blueberry pie filling	2 (567 g)
½ cup (1 stick) butter, softened	120 ml
1 (18 ounce) box white cake mix	510 g
1 egg	

+ In 9 x 13-inch (23 x 33 cm) baking pan, spread pie filling to cover bottom.
+ In large bowl, cream butter to smooth texture. Add dry cake mix and egg and blend well. (Mixture will be very stiff.)
+ Spoon mixture over pie filling.
+ Bake at 350° (176° C) for 40 minutes or until golden brown. Cut into 3-inch (7.5 cm) squares.

Berry Blue Cobbler

½ cup (1 stick) butter, melted	120 ml
1 cup self-rising flour	240 ml
1¾ cups sugar	420 ml
1 cup milk	240 ml
1 (20 ounce) can blueberry pie filling	567 g

+ Pour butter into 9-inch (23 cm) baking pan.
+ Mix flour and sugar in bowl. Slowly pour milk into flour mixture and stir.
+ Pour mixture over butter and spoon pie filling over batter.
+ Bake at 300° (148° C) for 1 hour. Top with whipped cream to serve.

Blueberry Cobbler

2 (20 ounce) cans blueberry pie filling	2 (567 g)
1 (18 ounce) box white cake mix	510 g
1 egg	
½ cup (1 stick) butter, softened	120 ml

+ Spread pie filling into greased 9 x 13-inch (23 x 33 cm) baking dish.
+ With mixer, combine cake mix, egg and butter and blend well. (Mixture will be stiff.)
+ Spoon batter over pie filling.
+ Bake at 350° (176° C) for 45 minutes or until golden brown.

Lightning Fast Peach Cobbler

½ cup (1 stick) butter	120 ml
1 (20 ounce) can sliced peaches, drained	567 g
1 cup milk	240 ml
1 cup sugar	240 ml
1 cup flour	240 ml

+ Preheat oven to 350° (176° C).
+ Melt butter in 9 x 13-inch (23 x 33 cm) baking dish. Place peaches on butter.
+ In medium bowl, combine milk, sugar and flour and pour mixture over peaches.
+ Bake for 1 hour.

Optional: Sprinkle 1 teaspoon (5 ml) cinnamon over peaches before adding milk mixture.

Special Peach Crisp

4¾ cups peeled, sliced peaches	1.1 L
3 tablespoons lemon juice	45 ml
1 cup flour	240 ml
1¾ cups sugar	420 ml
1 egg, beaten	

+ Place peaches in 9-inch (23 cm) baking dish and sprinkle lemon juice over top.
+ Mix flour, sugar, egg and a dash of salt. Spread mixture over top of peaches and dot with a little butter.
+ Bake at 375° (190° C) until golden brown.

Peachy Amaretto Crunch

2 (20 ounce) cans peach pie filling	2 (567 g)
½ cup amaretto liqueur	120 ml
1 (18 ounce) box white cake mix	510 g
1 cup slivered almonds, toasted	240 ml
½ cup (1 stick) butter	120 ml

+ Preheat oven to 350° (176° C).
+ Spread pie filling evenly in bottom of greased 9 x 13-inch (23 x 33 cm) baking dish and pour amaretto over filling.
+ Sprinkle cake mix evenly over top of filling and sprinkle with almonds.
+ Cut butter into ⅛-inch (.3 cm) slices and place over surface of cake mixture.
+ Bake for 40 to 45 minutes or until top is brown.

Peach Crumb

1 (20 ounce) can peach pie filling	567 g
½ cup quick-cooking oats	120 ml
½ cup flour	120 ml
½ cup firmly packed brown sugar	120 ml
½ cup (1 stick) butter, melted	120 ml

+ Preheat oven to 350° (176° C).
+ Pour peach pie filling in 8 x 8-inch (20 x 20 cm) baking dish.
+ In medium bowl, combine oats, flour and brown sugar. Stir in butter until mixture is thoroughly blended.
+ Sprinkle mixture evenly over peach pie filling.
+ Bake for 40 to 45 minutes or until topping is brown.

Cinnamon-Apple Cobbler

2 (20 ounce) cans apple pie filling	2 (567 g)
½ cup packed brown sugar	120 ml
1½ teaspoons cinnamon	7 ml
1 (18 ounce) box yellow cake mix	567 g
½ cup (1 stick) butter, melted	120 ml

+ Preheat oven to 350° (176° C).
+ Spread apple pie filling in bottom of greased
  9 x 13-inch (23 x 33 cm) baking dish.
+ Sprinkle with brown sugar and cinnamon and top with
  dry cake mix.
+ Drizzle melted butter over top of cake mix.
+ Bake for 50 minutes or until light brown and bubbly.

Cherry-Cinnamon Cobbler

1 (20 ounce) can cherry pie filling	567 g
1 (12 ounce) tube refrigerated cinnamon rolls	340 g

+ Spread pie filling into greased 8-inch (20 cm) baking
  dish.
+ Set aside icing from cinnamon rolls and arrange rolls
  around edge of baking dish.
+ Bake at 400° (204° C) for 15 minutes. Cover and bake
  another 10 minutes.
+ Spread icing over rolls and serve warm.

Cherry Crisp

2 (20 ounce) cans cherry pie filling	2 (567 g)
1 (18 ounce) box white cake mix	510 g
½ cup (1 stick) butter	120 ml
2 cups chopped pecans	480 ml

- Pour pie filling into greased 9 x 13-inch (23 x 33 cm) baking dish.
- Sprinkle cake mix over top of filling.
- Dot cake mix with butter and cover with pecans.
- Bake, uncovered, at 350° (176° C) for 45 minutes.

Cherry Cobbler

2 (20 ounce) cans cherry pie filling	2 (567 g)
1 (18 ounce) box white cake mix	510 g
¾ cup (1½ sticks) butter, melted	180 ml
1 (4 ounce) package slivered almonds	114 g

- Spread pie filling in greased 9 x 13-inch (23 x 33 cm) baking pan.
- Sprinkle cake mix over pie filling.
- Drizzle butter over top and sprinkle with almonds.
- Bake at 350° (176° C) for 45 minutes.
- Top with whipped topping to serve.

Apple Cobbler

2 (20 ounce) cans apple pie filling	2 (567 g)
2 cups biscuit mix	480 ml
½ cup (1 stick) butter	120 ml
1 cup milk	240 ml

Topping:

1 cup sugar	240 ml
¼ cup cornstarch	60 ml
1½ cups boiling water	360 ml

+ Preheat oven to 350° (176° C).
+ Place apple pie filling in buttered 9 x 13-inch (23 x 33 cm) baking dish.
+ Place biscuit mix in mixing bowl and cut in butter until crumbly. Stir in milk and spoon mixture over apples.
+ Combine sugar and cornstarch and sprinkle over batter.
+ Pour boiling water over mixture and bake, uncovered, for 45 minutes.

Apple Crisp

5 cups peeled, cored, sliced apples	1.3 ml
½ cup (1 stick) butter, melted	120 ml
1 cup quick-cooking oats	240 ml
½ cup firmly packed brown sugar	120 ml
⅓ cup flour	80 ml

+ Preheat over to 375° (190° C).
+ Place apple slices in 8 x 8-inch (20 x 20 cm) or
  9 x 9-inch (23 x 23 cm) square baking pan.
+ Combine butter, oats, brown sugar and flour and sprinkle
  mixture over apples.
+ Bake for 40 to 45 minutes or until apples are tender and
  topping is golden brown.

*Optional: Add 1 teaspoon (5 ml) cinnamon and
½ cup (120 ml) raisins or dried cranberries to apples
before sprinkling with topping.*

Lickity-Split Apple Crisp

This apple dish could not be easier. It is a great standby dessert if you keep the pie filling and oatmeal on hand. It can be put together in minutes, and there is little clean-up.

2 (20 ounce) cans apple pie filling	2 (567 g)
3 (1.6 ounce) packets cinnamon-spice	
instant oatmeal	3 (50 g)
½ cup flour	120 ml
¾ cup firmly packed brown sugar	180 ml
½ cup (1 stick) butter, melted	120 ml

- Preheat oven to 350° (176° C).
- Pour apple pie filling in 9 x 13-inch (23 x 33 cm) baking dish.
- Combine oatmeal, flour and brown sugar in bowl. Stir in melted butter and mix well.
- Crumble mixture over pie filling.
- Bake for 45 minutes or until top is golden brown.

For additional flavor, sprinkle 1 teaspoon (5 ml) apple pie spice over apple pie filling before the topping. You may also add ½ cup (120 ml) chopped pecans to the topping mixture. And last but not least, serve it warm with a scoop of vanilla ice cream for the ultimate taste treat.

Apple Tarts

1 (10 ounce) package frozen puff pastry shells	280 g
½ cup craisins (sweetened, dried cranberries)	120 ml
¼ cup apple brandy	60 ml
¼ cup sugar	60 ml
1 (20 ounce) can apple pie filling	567 g
½ teaspoon cinnamon	2 ml

- Preheat oven to 400° (204° C).
- Place pastry shells on ungreased baking sheet and bake for 20 minutes. Remove centers and cool.
- In saucepan, combine craisins, apple brandy and sugar and soak for 10 minutes.
- Add pie filling and cinnamon to saucepan and mix well. Fill each pastry shell with pie mixture.

If you like, serve the tarts with a dollop of whipped topping or a scoop of vanilla ice cream.

Fresh Peach Tarts

1 (8 ounce, 8 count) package frozen tart shells, thawed	227 g
⅔ cup ground pecans plus 8 pecan halves	160 ml
7 tablespoons lightly packed brown sugar, divided	105 ml
2 tablespoons (¼ stick) butter, melted	30 ml
2 large, firm, ripe peaches	

+ Preheat oven to 375° (190° C).
+ Put tart shells on baking sheet and bake for 5 minutes. Remove from oven and set aside.
+ Increase heat to 400° (204° C). Place pecans in small bowl and add 6 tablespoons (90 ml) brown sugar and butter. Stir well and set aside.
+ Slice peaches into ¼-inch (.6 cm) wedges and cut wedges in half to make pieces small enough to fit easily into tart shells. Combine with remaining 1 tablespoon (15 ml) brown sugar and stir until peaches are coated.
+ Divide peach mixture among tart shells.
+ Spoon pecan topping evenly over peaches. Place whole pecan half on top of each for garnish.
+ Bake 15 minutes or until topping and edges of tart are golden brown. Remove from oven and cool to room temperature before serving.

Fresh Lemon Tarts

1 (8 ounce, 8 count) package frozen tart shells	227 g
⅔ cup fresh lemon juice	160 ml
½ cup sugar	120 ml
3 tablespoons sour cream	45 ml
4 eggs	

+ Bake tart shells according to package directions. Set aside to cool.
+ Preheat oven to 375° (190° C).
+ Whisk lemon juice and sugar in medium bowl. Whisk in sour cream.
+ Add eggs 2 at a time and whisk until mixture blends well. Pour mixture into tart shells.
+ Bake tarts until filling is set, about 30 minutes. Cool tarts completely on cooling rack and chill at least 1 hour.

Optional: Garnish each tart with dollop of whipped cream and lemon slices.

Lemony Cheese Tarts

2 large lemons	
1 (8 ounce, 8 count) package	
frozen tart shells, thawed	227 g
3 eggs	
¾ cup sugar, divided	180 ml
1 (8 ounce) container mascarpone cheese,	
softened	227 g

+ Bake tart shells according to package directions. Set aside to cool.
+ Squeeze ½ cup (120 ml) juice from lemons and grate 1 tablespoon (15 ml) zest from peel. Set aside.
+ Beat eggs lightly and place in top of double boiler. Whisk in ½ cup (120 ml) sugar, lemon juice and lemon zest.
+ Cook in double boiler over simmering water, whisking constantly, until mixture is smooth and slightly thick, about 10 minutes. (The mixture is ready when it coats back of spoon and makes trail when you run your finger across it.)
+ Remove top of double boiler from heat and set aside to cool.
+ In medium bowl, beat cheese until light and fluffy. Gradually beat in remaining ¼ cup (60 ml) sugar.
+ Fold cooled lemon mixture into cheese mixture in several additions. Chill and divide among prepared tart shells.

Lime-Cheesecake Tarts

2 small limes	
1 (8 ounce) package cream cheese, softened	**227 g**
⅓ cup sugar	**80 ml**
1 egg	
1 (4 ounce, 6 count) package miniature	
graham cracker piecrusts, unbaked	**114 g**

+ Squeeze 3 tablespoons (45 ml) lime juice, grate
  1 teaspoon (5 ml) zest from peel and set aside.
+ Preheat oven to 325° (162° C).
+ In mixing bowl, beat cream cheese until smooth. Add
  sugar and beat until light and fluffy.
+ Beat in egg, then lime juice and lime zest.
+ Spoon cheese mixture into piecrusts and bake for 30 to
  35 minutes or until knife inserted in center comes out
  clean. Remove from oven and cool. Chill until ready to
  serve.

  *Optional: Serve with dollop of whipped cream and
  sprinkle of lime zest on top.*

Strawberry-Zabaglione Tarts

Zabaglione (also spelled Zabaione) is a rich Italian custard made from egg yolks, sugar and marsala wine. The light, frothy custard is perfect served as a sauce over cake, fruit, ice cream or pastry.

6 egg yolks	
½ cup sugar	**120 ml**
4 tablespoons sweet marsala wine	**60 ml**
1½ cups sliced strawberries	**360 ml**
1 (8 ounce, 8 count) package frozen tart	
shells, baked, cooled	**227 g**

+ Whisk egg yolks and sugar in medium bowl until well blended and whisk in wine.
+ Place mixture in top of double boiler over simmering water and whisk vigorously and constantly until mixture increases in volume and thickens.
+ Scrape sides of pan frequently as you whisk. (Make sure water does not boil to avoid eggs curdling.) Mixture is cooked when it coats whisk.
+ Remove from heat and cool slightly.
+ Place strawberries in tart shells and spoon custard over strawberries. Chill until ready to serve. (This dish may be made several hours in advance.)

Tip: Frozen tarts will be with the frozen piecrusts in grocery store.

Strawberry-Lemon Curd Tartlets

These tartlets are 5-minute wonders!

1 (8 ounce, 8 count) package frozen tart shells, baked, cooled	227 g
2 cups lemon curd	480 ml
1 pint fresh strawberries, sliced	.5 kg
¼ cup seedless strawberry jam	60 ml

+ Buy prepared lemon curd or prepare lemon curd recipe on page 165.
+ Divide lemon curd among baked tart shells.
+ Place strawberry slices attractively on top.
+ Warm strawberry jam in microwave on MEDIUM HIGH for about 45 seconds and brush jam over strawberries with pastry brush for glaze.
+ Serve immediately.

Cakes

Mom's Pound Cake

1 cup (2 sticks) butter, softened	240 ml
2 cups sugar	480 ml
5 eggs	
2 cups flour	480 ml
1 tablespoon almond flavoring	15 ml

+ Preheat oven to 325° (162° C).
+ Combine all ingredients in mixing bowl and beat for 10 minutes at medium speed. (Batter will be very thick.)
+ Pour into greased, floured tube pan.
+ Bake for 1 hour. Test with toothpick for doneness.

Fancy Pound Cake

1 (10 ounce) bakery pound cake	280 g
1 (15 ounce) can crushed pineapple with juice	425 g
1 (3.4 ounce) package instant coconut	
pudding mix	98 g
1 (8 ounce) carton whipped topping	227 g
½ cup flaked coconut	120 ml

+ Slice cake horizontally into 3 equal layers.
+ Mix pineapple, pudding mix and whipped topping and blend well.
+ Spread pineapple mixture on each layer and sprinkle top of cake with coconut.
+ Chill before serving.

Extreme Pound Cake

1 (9 inch) round bakery pound cake	23 cm
1 (20 ounce) can crushed pineapple with juice	567 g
1 (3.4 ounce) instant vanilla pudding mix	98 g
1 (8 ounce) carton whipped topping, divided	227 g

+ Cut pound cake horizontally into 3 equal layers and place bottom layer on cake plate.
+ In bowl, gently combine and mix pineapple and pudding mix. When well mixed, fold in half whipped topping.
+ Spread one-third pineapple mixture over top of bottom layer (not on sides). Place second layer on top and spread half remaining pineapple mixture. Top with third cake layer and remaining pineapple mixture.
+ Top with remaining whipped topping and refrigerate.

Cakes

Lemon Pound Cake

2 cups sugar	480 ml
1 cup (2 sticks) butter	240 ml
6 eggs	
2 cups flour	480 ml
1 teaspoon lemon extract	5 ml

+ Preheat oven to 350° (176° C).
+ Cream sugar and butter until light and fluffy.
+ Add eggs one at a time and beat well after each addition. Gradually add flour and lemon extract.
+ Pour batter into greased tube or bundt pan and bake for 50 to 60 minutes. Cake is done when toothpick or cake tester is inserted in center and comes out clean.
+ Serve with Raspberry Sauce (page 265) spooned over each slice.

Quick Summer Cake

1 (16 ounce) frozen loaf pound cake	.5 kg
1 (8 ounce) carton whipping cream	227 g
1 (20 ounce) can coconut pie filling	567 g
2 kiwi fruit, peeled, sliced	

+ Slice cake horizontally into 3 equal layers and place bottom layer on serving platter.
+ With mixer, beat whipping cream until thick, fold in pie filling and mix until they blend well.
+ Spread one-third whipped cream mixture over bottom cake layer. Place second layer on top and spread with half remaining whipped cream mixture. Top with third cake layer and spread remaining whipped cream mixture on top.
+ Garnish cake with slices of kiwi and refrigerate.

Blueberry Pound Cake

1 (18 ounce) box yellow cake mix	510 g
1 (8 ounce) package cream cheese, softened	227 g
½ cup oil	120 ml
4 eggs	
1 (15 ounce) can whole blueberries, drained	425 ml

+ Preheat oven to 350° (176° C).
+ Combine all ingredients and beat for 3 minutes with mixer.
+ Pour batter into greased, floured bundt or tube pan.
+ Bake at 350° (176° C) for 50 minutes. Test with toothpick to be sure cake is done.
+ Sprinkle powdered sugar over top of cake.

Strawberry Pound Cake

1 (18 ounce) box strawberry cake mix	510 g
1 (3.4 ounce) package instant pineapple pudding mix	98 g
⅓ cup oil	
4 eggs	
1 (3 ounce) package strawberry gelatin mix	84 g

+ Preheat oven to 350° (176° C).
+ Mix all ingredients plus 1 cup water and beat for 2 minutes at medium speed.
+ Pour into greased, floured bundt pan.
+ Bake for 55 to 60 minutes. Cake is done when toothpick inserted in center comes out clean.
+ Cool for 20 minutes before removing cake from pan. If you would like an icing, use commercial vanilla icing.

If you like coconut better than pineapple, use coconut cream pudding mix.

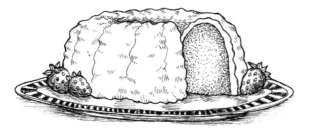

Strawberry Shortcakes

2½ cups biscuit mix	600 ml
¼ cup sugar	60 ml
3 tablespoons butter, softened	45 ml
½ cup milk	120 ml
1 (8 ounce) carton whipped topping	227 g

Strawberry Glaze:

1 tablespoon cornstarch	15 ml
1 teaspoon almond extract	5 ml
¾ cup sugar	180 ml
1 (16 ounce) container frozen strawberries, thawed	.5 kg

+ Preheat oven to 350° (176° C).
+ In mixing bowl, combine biscuit mix and sugar and cut in butter until mixture is crumbly. Add milk and stir just until soft dough forms.
+ Drop heaping tablespoons of batter onto greased baking sheet. Bake about 15 minutes or until light brown.
+ To make glaze, place cornstarch, almond extract, sugar and 2 tablespoons (30 ml) water in saucepan.
+ Add strawberries, bring mixture to boil and stir constantly. Reduce heat, cook and stir until mixture thickens. Remove from heat and chill.
+ When ready to serve, split shortcakes in half and spoon about ½ cup (120 ml) Strawberry Glaze over bottom half of each shortcake. Top with an ample amount of whipped topping and place top half of shortcake on top. Spoon remaining glaze over top.

Cakes

Shortcakes for Strawberries or Raspberries

2½ cups plus 2 tablespoons flour	600 ml
2½ teaspoons baking powder	12 ml
⅓ cup sugar	80 ml
½ cup (1 stick) butter, softened, sliced	120 ml
1 cup milk	240 ml

+ Preheat oven to 400° (204° C).
+ In bowl, combine flour, baking powder, sugar and butter. Stir and mix with fork until mixture resembles coarse meal.
+ Add milk and mix until dough forms. Place dough on lightly floured surface and, with lightly floured hands, pat dough into 4 x 6-inch (4 x 15 cm) rectangle.
+ Cut dough into 8 squares and place on greased baking sheet.
+ Bake 30 minutes or until light brown.
+ To serve, cut biscuits in half and serve with sugared strawberries or raspberries and top with whipped topping.

Strawberry-Angel Delight Cake

1 cup sweetened condensed milk	240 ml
¼ cup lemon juice	60 ml
1 pint fresh strawberries, halved	.5 kg
1 prepared bakery angel food cake	
1 pint whipping cream, whipped	.5 kg

- Combine condensed milk and lemon juice. Fold in strawberries.
- Slice cake horizontally to make 2 layers. Spread strawberry filling on bottom layer and place top layer over filling.
- Cover with whipped cream and top with extra strawberries.

Caramel-Angel Cake

This easy 5-minute recipe will make people think you are an angel!

1 cup packed brown sugar	240 ml
3 cups whipping cream, chilled	710 ml
1 (20 ounce) can crushed pineapple, well drained	567 g
½ cup ground pecans	120 ml
1 prepared bakery angel food cake	

- Mix brown sugar and whipping cream in large bowl and stir well.
- Beat whipping cream mixture until peaks form. Gently fold in pineapple and pecans.
- Slice angel food cake into 3 equal layers and spread each layer, sides and top, with whipped cream mixture.
- Chill 12 to 24 hours before serving.

Cakes

Creamy Surprise Cake

1 prepared bakery angel food cake	
1 (18 ounce) jar chocolate ice cream topping	510 g
½ gallon vanilla ice cream, softened	1.5 L
1 (12 ounce) carton whipped topping	340 g
½ cup slivered almonds, toasted	120 ml

- Tear cake into large pieces. Stir in chocolate topping to coat pieces of cake.
- Mix in softened ice cream. (Work fast.) Place in tube pan and freeze overnight.
- Turn cake out onto large cake plate and frost with whipped topping. Decorate with almonds and freeze again before serving.

All-You-Can-Eat Chocolate Cake

1 (18 ounce) box chocolate cake mix	510 g
1 cup mayonnaise	240 ml
3 eggs, slightly beaten	
1 teaspoon cinnamon	5 ml
1 cup water	240 ml
2 (16 ounce) cartons prepared chocolate icing	2 (.5 kg)

- Preheat oven to 350° (176° C).
- In mixing bowl, beat all ingredients. Pour batter into 2 (9 inch/23 cm) cake pans and bake cake according to package directions.
- Spread 1 carton prepared icing over each layer.

5-Minute Candy Bar Cake

This easy, layered cake has the flavor of an Almond Joy candy bar. I like to frost only the top of the cake so you see the layers.

1 (16 ounce) frozen pound cake, thawed	.5 kg
1 (7 ounce) package flaked coconut	198 g
1 (14 ounce) can sweetened condensed milk	396 g
½ cup chopped almonds, toasted	120 ml
1 (16 ounce) carton prepared chocolate fudge frosting	.5 kg

+ Split pound cake horizontally into 4 equal layers. (It is easier to slice cake when cake is very cold.)
+ In small bowl, combine coconut and sweetened condensed milk. Stir until they blend well.
+ Spread half coconut mixture on bottom cake layer. Sprinkle half almonds.
+ Place second cake layer on top and spread with chocolate frosting.
+ Repeat layers.

Super Oreo Cake

1 (18 ounce) box white cake mix	510 g
⅓ cup oil	80 ml
4 egg whites	
1¼ cups coarsely crushed chocolate-sandwich cookies	300 ml

- Grease and flour 2 (8 or 9 inch/23 cm) round cake pans and set aside.
- Preheat oven to 350° (176° C).
- In large mixing bowl, combine cake mix, 1¼ cups (300 ml) water, oil and egg whites and blend on slow speed until moist. Beat 2 minutes on high speed.
- Gently fold in crushed cookies and pour batter into prepared pans.
- Bake for 25 to 30 minutes or until toothpick inserted in center comes out clean.
- Cool 10 minutes and remove from pan. Cool completely.

Frosting:

4¼ cups powdered sugar	1.2 L
1 cup (2 sticks) butter, softened	240 ml
1 cup shortening	240 ml
1 teaspoon almond extract	5 ml
½ cup crushed chocolate-sandwich cookies	120 ml

- Beat powdered sugar, butter, shortening and almond extract with mixer.
- Spread frosting on first layer of cake and put second layer on top.
- Spread frosting over top layer and sprinkle with crushed cookies.

Optional: About ¾ cup (180 ml) chopped pecans are great sprinkled over the top of this cake.

Banana-Butter Cake

1 (18 ounce) box yellow cake mix	510 g
2 ripe bananas	
3 (2 ounce) Butterfinger candy bars, chopped, divided	3 (57 g)
½ cup chopped pecans	120 ml
1 (16 ounce) carton prepared white frosting	.5 kg

+ Preheat over to 350° (176° C).
+ Prepare cake batter according to package directions.
+ Mash bananas and stir into batter. Fold in about ¾ cup (180 ml) chopped Butterfinger and chopped pecans.
+ Pour into greased, floured 9 x 13-inch (23 x 33 cm) baking pan.
+ Bake for 40 to 50 minutes or until toothpick inserted in center comes out clean.
+ Cool thoroughly, remove from pan and spread with frosting. Sprinkle remaining chopped Butterfinger over top.

Delightful Pear Cake

1 (15 ounce) can pears in light syrup with juice	425 g
1 (18 ounce) box white cake mix	510 g
2 egg whites	
1 egg	

+ Preheat oven to 350° (176° C).
+ Drain pears, save liquid and chop pears.
+ Place pears and liquid in mixing bowl and add cake mix, egg whites and egg. Beat on LOW speed for 30 seconds. Beat on HIGH for 4 minutes.
+ Pour batter into greased, floured 10-inch bundt pan.
+ Bake at 350° (176° C) for 50 to 55 minutes and cook until toothpick inserted in middle comes out clean.
+ Cool in pan for 10 minutes, remove cake and dust with sifted powdered sugar.

Cranberry Coffee Cake

2 eggs
1 cup mayonnaise   240 ml
1 (18 ounce) box spice cake mix   510 g
1 (16 ounce) can whole cranberry sauce   .5 kg
Powdered sugar

- In mixing bowl, beat eggs, mayonnaise and cake mix and mix well. Fold in cranberry sauce.
- Pour into greased, floured 9 x 13-inch (23 x 33 cm) baking pan.
- Bake at 325° (162° C) for 45 minutes. Test with toothpick to be sure cake is done.
- When cake is cool, dust with powdered sugar. (If you would rather have icing instead of powdered sugar, use a prepared icing.)

Cherry Cake

1 (18 ounce) box French vanilla cake mix   510 g
½ cup (1 stick) butter, melted   120 ml
2 eggs
1 (20 ounce) can cherry pie filling   567 g
1 cup chopped pecans   240 ml

- Preheat oven to 350° (176° C).
- In large bowl, mix all ingredients by hand.
- Pour into greased, floured bundt or tube pan.
- Bake for 1 hour.
- Sprinkle powdered sugar on top of cake if you like.

Chocolate-Cherry Cake

1 (18 ounce) box milk chocolate cake mix	510 g
1 (20 ounce) can cherry pie filling	567 g
3 eggs	

- ✦ Preheat oven to 350° (176° C).
- ✦ Combine cake mix, pie filling and eggs in mixing bowl and mix by hand.
- ✦ Pour into greased, floured 9 x 13-inch (23 x 33 cm) baking pan.
- ✦ Bake for 35 to 40 minutes. Test cake for doneness with toothpick.

Frosting:

5 tablespoons (⅔ stick) butter	75 ml
1¼ cups sugar	300 ml
½ cup milk	120 ml
1 (6 ounce) package chocolate chips	168 g

- ✦ Combine butter, sugar and milk in medium saucepan.
- ✦ Bring to boil and cook for 1 minute, stirring constantly.
- ✦ Add chocolate chips and stir until chips melt.
- ✦ Pour over hot cake.

Cherry-Nut Cake

1(18 ounce) box French vanilla cake mix	510 g
½ cup (1 stick) butter, melted	120 ml
2 eggs	
1 (20 ounce) can cherry pie filling	567 g
1 cup chopped pecans	240 ml

+ In large bowl, mix all ingredients by hand.
+ Pour into greased, floured bundt or tube pan.
+ Bake at 350° (176° C) for 1 hour. (Sprinkle some powdered sugar on top of cake if you would like a sweeter cake.)

Cherry-Pineapple Cake

1 (20 ounce) can crushed pineapple, drained	567 g
1 (20 ounce) can cherry pie filling	567 g
1 (18 ounce) box yellow cake mix	510 g
1 cup (2 sticks) butter, softened	240 ml
1¼ cups chopped pecans	300 ml

+ Place all ingredients in mixing bowl and mix by hand.
+ Pour into greased, floured 9 x 13-inch (23 x 33 cm) baking dish.
+ Bake at 350° (176° C) for 1 hour 10 minutes.

Pineapple Upside-Down Cake

½ cup (1 stick) butter	120 ml
2 cups packed light brown sugar	480 ml
1 (20 ounce) can crushed pineapple, drained	567 g
10 maraschino cherries, quartered	
1 (18 ounce) box pineapple cake mix	510 g

+ Preheat oven to 350° (176° C).
+ In small saucepan, melt butter and brown sugar until creamy. Divide mixture evenly between 2 greased, floured 9-inch (23 cm) cake pans.
+ Spread pineapple and cherries evenly over brown sugar mixture in each pan.
+ Prepare cake batter according to package directions and pour over pineapple.
+ Bake for 35 to 40 minutes or until toothpick inserted in center of cake comes out clean.
+ Remove cake from oven and cool for 10 minutes.
+ Put plate on top of cake pan, turn cake pan upside down and tap bottom of cake pan several times with knife. Gently lift cake pan off cake.

Hawaiian Pineapple Cake

1 (20 ounce) can crushed pineapple, drained	567 g
1 (20 ounce) can cherry pie filling	567 g
1 (18 ounce) box yellow cake mix	510 g
1 cup (2 sticks) butter, softened	240 ml
1¼ cups chopped pecans	300 ml

- Place all ingredients in large bowl and mix by hand.
- Pour into greased, floured 9 x 13-inch (23 x 33 cm) baking dish.
- Bake at 350° (176° C) for 1 hour 10 minutes.

Brandy-Spiced Peach Cake

1 (20 ounce) can peach pie filling	567 g
1 (18 ounce) box yellow cake mix	510 g
3 eggs	
½ cup brandy	120 ml
¼ cup vegetable oil	60 ml

- In blender, process pie filling until smooth.
- In large bowl, combine pie filling, dry cake mix, eggs, brandy and oil and blend well.
- Pour into greased, floured 10-inch (25 cm) tube pan.
- Bake at 350° (176° C) for 1 hour or until cake springs back when lightly touched.

Optional: Sprinkle with powdered sugar before serving.

Peaches 'n Cream

1 (18 ounce) box yellow cake mix	510 g
½ cup (1 stick) butter, melted	120 ml
3 eggs, divided	
1 (20 ounce) can peach pie filling	567 g
1 pint sour cream	.5 kg

+ In large bowl, combine dry cake mix, butter and 2 eggs and blend well.
+ Pour into 9 x 13-inch baking pan.
+ Bake at 350° (176° C) for 25 minutes. Remove from oven.
+ Spoon pie filling over cake.
+ In small bowl, combine sour cream and remaining egg.
+ Pour mixture over pie filling.
+ Bake another 15 minutes or until sour cream topping sets. Cut into 3-inch (7.5 cm) squares.

Chocolate-Orange Cake

1 (16 ounce) loaf frozen pound cake, thawed	.5 kg
1 (12 ounce) jar orange marmalade	340 g
1 (16 ounce) carton prepared	
chocolate-fudge frosting	.5 kg

+ Cut cake horizontally into 3 equal layers.
+ Place 1 layer on cake platter and spread with half marmalade.
+ Place second layer over first and spread with remaining marmalade.
+ Top with third cake layer and spread frosting liberally on top and sides of cake.
+ Chill.

Creamy Orange Chiffon Cake

Everyone is surprised by how easy and how good this cake is!

1 prepared bakery orange chiffon cake
1 (15 ounce) can crushed pineapple with juice   425 g
1 (3.4 ounce) package instant
   vanilla pudding mix   100 g
1 (8 ounce) carton whipped topping   227 g
½ cup slivered almonds, toasted   120 ml

- Slice cake horizontally into 3 equal layers.
- Combine pineapple, pudding mix and whipped topping and mix well.
- Spread pineapple mixture on each layer and cover top of cake. Sprinkle almonds on top. Refrigerate.

Quick, Easy Fruitcake

1 (15.6 ounce) package cranberry or
   blueberry quick-bread mix   430 g
½ cup chopped pecans   120 ml
½ cup chopped dates   120 ml
¼ cup chopped maraschino cherries   60 ml
¼ cup crushed pineapple, drained   60 ml

- Prepare quick-bread batter according to package directions.
- Stir in remaining ingredients. Pour into greased 9 x 5-inch (23 x 13 cm) loaf pan.
- Bake at 350° (176° C) for 60 minutes or until toothpick inserted in cake comes out clean.
- Cool 10 minutes before removing from pan.

Cakes

Lemony Sponge Cake

4 eggs
1 (18 ounce) box yellow cake mix   510 g
½ cup plus 2 tablespoons vegetable oil   120 ml; 30 ml
3 teaspoons lemon extract   15 ml
⅔ cup apricot nectar   160 ml

+ Preheat oven to 350°(176° C).
+ In small bowl, crack eggs and beat slightly to mix.
+ In large bowl, combine dry cake mix and eggs until eggs are absorbed into mixture.
+ Pour in oil, lemon extract and apricot nectar and mix well.
+ Pour batter into greased, floured cake pan.
+ Bake for 40 to 45 minutes.

Optional: A lemon glaze is wonderful poured over the top of this cake. Mix the juice of 2 lemons and 1½ cups (360 ml) powdered sugar until smooth and pour over cake after it has cooled slightly.

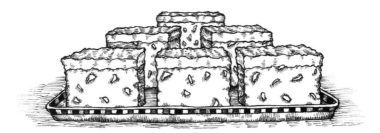

Cakes
Lemon-Poppy Seed Cake

1 (18 ounce) box lemon cake mix with pudding	510 g
1 (8 ounce) carton sour cream	227 g
3 eggs	
⅓ cup oil	80 ml
⅓ cup poppy seeds	80 ml

- Preheat oven to 350° (176° C).
- Prepare 12-cup (3 L) bundt pan with non-stick spray. (Use spray that already contains flour.)
- In mixing bowl, combine dry cake mix, sour cream, eggs, oil and ¼ cup (60 ml) water and beat on medium speed until ingredients mix well.
- Stir in poppy seeds and mix until seeds are evenly distributed. Pour batter into prepared bundt pan.
- Bake for 45 minutes and test for doneness with toothpick. Cool.

If you like, you can dust cake with powdered sugar or spread prepared vanilla icing on top of cake.

 Cakes

Grandma's Strawberry Cake

1 (18 ounce) box strawberry cake mix	510 g
1 (3.4 ounce) package instant coconut cream pudding mix	98 g
⅓ cup oil	80 ml
4 eggs	
1 (3 ounce) package strawberry gelatin mix	84 g

+ Mix all ingredients plus 1 cup (240 ml) water and beat for 2 minutes at medium speed.
+ Pour into greased, floured bundt pan.
+ Bake at 325° (176° C) for 55 to 60 minutes. Cake is done when toothpick inserted into center comes out clean.
+ Cool for 20 minutes before removing cake from pan.

Carnival Cake

1 (18 ounce) box white cake mix	510 g
2 (10 ounce) packages frozen, sweetened strawberries with juice	2 (280 ml)
1 (3.4 ounce) package instant vanilla pudding mix	98 g
1 (8 ounce) carton whipped topping	227 g

+ Mix and bake white cake according to package directions.
+ When cool, poke holes in cake with knife and pour strawberries over top.
+ Prepare vanilla pudding using 1¼ cups (300 ml) milk. When set, spread pudding over strawberries.
+ Cover cake with whipped topping and refrigerate.

Fruit Cocktail Cake

2 cups sugar	480 ml
2 cups flour	480 ml
1 teaspoon baking soda	5 ml
2 (15 ounce) cans fruit cocktail, divided	2 (425 g)

+ Preheat oven to 350° (176° C).
+ With mixer, combine sugar, flour, baking soda, 1 can fruit cocktail with juice and half other can fruit cocktail, but drain this can. (Reserve half can fruit cocktail.)
+ Beat several minutes with mixer (fruit will be chopped up).
+ Pour into greased, floured 9 x 13-inch (23 x 33 cm) baking pan and bake for 30 to 35 minutes. Test with toothpick to make sure cake is done.
+ While cake is cooking, prepare icing.

Fruit Cocktail Cake Icing:

1 (8 ounce) package cream cheese, softened	227 g
½ cup (1 stick) butter, softened	120 ml
Reserved drained fruit cocktail	
Flaked coconut	
Powdered sugar	

+ Combine cream cheese and butter and beat until creamy.
+ Add remaining fruit, coconut and powdered sugar.
+ Beat several minutes until fruit chops well and pour mixture over hot cake.
+ When cool, store in refrigerator.

Tip: Pecans may be substituted for coconut.

Fresh Berry Cake

This is a fun 5-minute recipe because you may use any combination of berries and fruit.

1 prepared bakery angel food cake	
⅔ cup strawberry jam, divided	**160 ml**
2½ cups fresh blueberries, rinsed,	
** drained, divided**	**600 ml**
1 (8 ounce) carton whipped topping, divided	**227 g**
1 pint strawberries, hulled, sliced	**.5 kg**

- Slice angel food cake in half horizontally.
- Place bottom layer on serving plate and spread ⅓ cup (80 ml) jam on top. Arrange 1 cup (240 ml) blueberries over jam.
- Spread half whipped topping over blueberries to within ½ inch (1.2 cm) of cake edge.
- Place second layer on top and spread with remaining jam.
- Arrange 1 cup (240 ml) blueberries over jam and spread remaining whipped topping over them.
- Arrange strawberry slices and remaining ½ cup (120 ml) blueberries attractively over whipped topping as garnish.
- Chill until ready to serve.

Deluxe Coconut Cake

1 (18 ounce) box yellow cake mix	510 g
1 (14 ounce) can sweetened condensed milk	396 g
1 (10 ounce) can coconut cream	280 g
1 (4 ounce) can flaked coconut	114 g
1 (8 ounce) carton whipped topping	227 g

+ Prepare cake batter according to package directions and pour into greased, floured 9 x 13-inch (23 x 33 cm) baking pan.
+ Bake at 350° (176° C) for 30 to 35 minutes or until toothpick inserted in center comes out clean.
+ While cake is warm, make holes in cake about 2 inches (5 cm) apart.
+ Pour sweetened condensed milk over cake and spread until all milk soaks into cake.
+ Pour coconut cream over cake and sprinkle coconut over top.
+ When cake is cool, frost with whipped topping. Chill before serving.

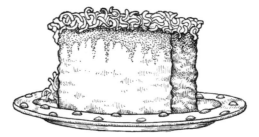

Pumpkin-Rum Cake

1 (18 ounce) box white cake mix	510 g
1 (15 ounce) can pumpkin	425 g
3 eggs	
½ cup rum	120 ml
¾ cup chopped pecans, toasted	160 ml

+ Preheat oven to 325° (162° C).
+ In large bowl, combine dry cake mix, pumpkin, eggs and rum. Beat on low speed to blend. Beat on medium speed for 2 minutes.
+ Fold in pecans and pour batter into greased, floured 12-cup (3 L) bundt pan.
+ Bake for 45 to 50 minutes or until cake tester comes out clean.
+ Cool 10 minutes. Turn out onto serving platter and frost with Orange Glaze.

Orange Glaze:

1 cup powdered sugar	240 ml
2 tablespoons plus ½ teaspoon orange juice	30 ml; 2 ml
1 tablespoon orange zest	15 ml

+ Mix all ingredients until smooth.
+ Spoon over top of cake and allow glaze to run down sides of cake.

Pumpkin Mini-Cakes

1 (18 ounce) box spice cake mix	510 g
1 (15 ounce) can pumpkin	425 g
3 eggs	
⅓ cup oil	80 ml
⅓ cup water	80 ml

- In mixing bowl, blend all ingredients. Beat for 2 minutes.
- Pour batter into 24 paper-lined muffin cups. Fill each cup three-fourths full.
- Bake at 350° (176° C) for 18 to 20 minutes or until toothpick inserted in center comes out clean. (If you want a sweeter cupcake, frost with prepared icing.)

Old-Fashioned Applesauce Cake

1 (18 ounce) box spice cake mix	510 g
3 eggs	
1¼ cups applesauce	300 ml
⅓ cup oil	80 ml
1 cup chopped pecans	240 ml

- With mixer, combine dry cake mix, eggs, applesauce and oil. Beat at medium speed for 2 minutes. Stir in pecans.
- Pour into greased, floured 9 x 13-inch (23 x 33 cm) baking pan.
- Bake at 350° (176° C) for 40 minutes. Test for doneness with toothpick and cool.
- For frosting, use prepared vanilla frosting and stir in ½ teaspoon (2 ml) cinnamon before spreading on cake.

Gooey Butter Cake

4 eggs, divided	
1 (18 ounce) box butter cake mix	**510 g**
½ cup (1 stick) butter, melted	**120 ml**
1 (16 ounce) box powdered sugar, divided	**.5 kg**
1 (8 ounce) package cream cheese, softened	**227 g**

+ Preheat oven to 350° (176° C).
+ With mixer, beat 2 eggs, cake mix and butter and spread mixture into greased, floured 9 x 13-inch (23 x 33 cm) baking pan.
+ Reserve ¾ cup (180 ml) powdered sugar for topping. Mix remaining powdered sugar, 2 remaining eggs and cream cheese and beat until smooth.
+ Spread mixture on top of batter and sprinkle reserved powdered sugar on top.
+ Bake cake for 40 minutes. Cake will puff up and then go down when it cools.

Golden Butter Cake

2 cups sugar	480 ml
1 cup (2 sticks) butter, softened	240 ml
3 eggs	
2 cups flour	480 ml
2 tablespoons orange juice	30 ml

- Preheat oven to 350° (176° C).
- Cream sugar and butter until light and fluffy. Add eggs one at a time and beat after each addition.
- Stir in flour and orange juice.
- Pour batter into greased, floured bundt or tube pan.
- Bake for about 1 hour. Cake is done when toothpick or cake tester inserted in center comes out clean.

Golden Rum Cake

1 (18 ounce) box yellow cake mix with pudding	510 g
3 eggs	
⅓ cup oil	80 ml
½ cup rum	120 ml
1 cup chopped pecans	240 ml

- Mix cake mix, eggs, oil, rum and 1⅓ cups (320 ml) water in mixing bowl and blend well.
- Stir in pecans. Pour into greased, floured 10-inch (25 cm) tube or bundt pan.
- Bake at 325° (162° C) for 1 hour. (If you want a sweeter cake, sprinkle powdered sugar over top of cooled cake.)

French Vanilla Cake

1 (18 ounce) box French vanilla cake mix	510 g
1 pint vanilla ice cream, softened	.5 kg
3 eggs, beaten	
1 teaspoon vanilla extract	5 ml

Icing:

1 (8 ounce) package cream cheese, softened	227 g
¼ cup (½ stick) butter, softened	60 ml
2 tablespoons kahlua	30 ml
1½ cups powdered sugar	360 ml

+ Preheat oven to 350° (176° C).
+ In mixing bowl, beat all cake ingredients for 3 minutes on medium speed. Spoon into greased, floured 10-inch (25 cm) bundt pan.
+ Bake for 35 to 40 minutes or until toothpick inserted in center comes out clean. Cool in pan for about 20 minutes and invert onto cake plate. Cool completely before icing.
+ In mixing bowl, beat cream cheese, butter and kahlua on low speed until light and creamy. Gradually add powdered sugar and beat for about 2 minutes.
+ Refrigerate icing until cake cools completely and spread icing on top and sides of cake.

Chess Cake

1 (18 ounce) box yellow cake mix	510 g
2 eggs	
½ cup (1 stick) butter, softened	120 ml

+ Beat cake mix, eggs and butter. Press into greased 9 x 13-inch (23 x 33 cm) baking pan.

Topping:

2 eggs	
1 (8 ounce) package cream cheese, softened	227 g
1 (16 ounce) box powdered sugar	.5 kg

+ Beat 2 eggs, cream cheese and powdered sugar. Pour topping mixture over cake batter.
+ Bake at 350° (176° C) for 35 minutes.

Favorite Cake

1 (18 ounce) box butter pecan cake mix	510 g
1 cup almond-toffee bits	240 ml
1 cup chopped pecans	240 ml
Powdered sugar	

+ Prepare cake batter according to package directions. Fold in almond-toffee bits and pecans.
+ Pour into greased, floured bundt pan.
+ Bake at 350° (176° C) for 45 minutes or until toothpick inserted in center comes out clean.
+ Allow cake to cool several minutes and remove cake from pan. Dust with sifted powdered sugar.

Cakes

White Chocolate-Almond Cake

1 (18 ounce) box white cake mix	510 g
4 egg whites	
¼ cup oil	60 ml
1 teaspoon almond extract	5 ml
1 cup chopped almonds	240 ml
6 (1 ounce) squares white chocolate, melted	6 (28 g)
1 (16 ounce) carton prepared caramel icing	.5 kg

+ Preheat oven to 350° (176° C).
+ In mixing bowl, combine cake mix, egg whites, oil, almond extract and 1½ cups (360 ml) water and beat until all ingredients blend well.
+ Stir in chopped almonds and melted white chocolate and pour into 2 (9 inch/23 cm) round cake pans.
+ Bake for 30 to 35 minutes or until toothpick inserted near center of cake comes out clean.
+ Spread each layer with half prepared icing. Place second layer on top of first layer.

Pecan Cake

1 (18 ounce) box butter pecan cake mix	510 g
½ cup (1 stick) butter, melted	120 ml
1 egg	
1 cup chopped pecans	240 ml

+ Combine cake mix, butter, egg and ¾ cup (180 ml) water.
+ Mix well and stir in pecans.
+ Pour into 9 x 13-inch (23 x 33 cm) baking dish.

Topping:

1 (8 ounce) package cream cheese, softened	227 g
2 eggs	
1 (1 pound) box powdered sugar	.5 kg

+ Use mixer to combine cream cheese, eggs and powdered sugar.
+ Pour topping over cake mixture and bake at 350° (176° C) for 40 minutes.

Poppy Seed Cake

1 (18 ounce) box yellow cake mix	510 g
1 (3.4 ounce) package instant coconut cream pudding mix	98 g
½ cup oil	120 ml
3 eggs	
2 tablespoons poppy seeds	30 ml

+ In mixing bowl, combine cake mix, pudding mix, oil, eggs and 1 cup (240 ml) water. Beat on low speed until moist. Beat on medium speed for 2 minutes.
+ Stir in poppy seeds. Pour into greased, floured bundt pan.
+ Bake at 350° (176° C) for 50 minutes or until toothpick inserted near the center comes out clean.
+ Cool for 10 minutes and remove from pan. Dust with powdered sugar.

Easy, Creamy Chocolate Torte

1 (10 ounce) frozen pound cake loaf	**280 g**
½ cup powdered sugar	**120 ml**
¼ cup cocoa	**60 ml**
1 cup whipping cream, chilled	**240 ml**
1 teaspoon vanilla extract	**5 ml**
Chocolate syrup	

- Allow cake to thaw and slice horizontally to make 4 layers.
- Combine sugar and cocoa in medium bowl. Pour in whipping cream and vanilla and beat until stiff peaks form.
- On serving platter, place first layer of cake and spread one-third whipped cream mixture over cake.
- Place second layer of cake on top and spread with another one-third whipped cream mixture.
- Repeat with another cake layer and remaining whipped cream mixture. Top with final layer of cake.
- Drizzle chocolate syrup over top and sides.

Easy Apricot Trifle Express

1 (18 ounce) box yellow cake mix	510 g
1 (20 ounce) can apricot pie filling	567 g
1 cup sliced almonds, toasted, divided	240 ml
2 cups whipped topping	480 ml

- Prepare and bake 2 (9 inch/23 cm) cake layers according to package directions.
- Break 1 cake layer into pieces. (Freeze remaining cake layer for another use.)
- Place half of cake pieces in 2-quart (2 L) serving bowl.
- In medium bowl, combine pie filling and ⅔ cup (160 ml) sliced almonds. Fold in whipped topping.
- Spoon half pie filling mixture over cake pieces. Repeat layer of cake pieces and remaining pie filling.
- Sprinkle with remaining almonds.
- Cover and chill at least 4 hours before serving.

Easy Cheesecake

2 (8 ounce) packages cream cheese, softened	2 (227 g)
½ cup sugar	120 ml
½ teaspoon vanilla extract	2 ml
2 eggs	
1 (9 inch) graham cracker piecrust	23 cm

- In mixing bowl, beat cream cheese, sugar, vanilla and eggs and pour into piecrust.
- Bake at 350° (176° C) for 40 minutes.
- Chill and serve as is or top with any canned pie filling.

Chocolate Cheesecake on Brownie Crust

1 (18 ounce) package ready-to-bake brownies	510 g
3 (8 ounce) packages cream cheese, softened	3 (227 g)
½ cup sugar	120 ml
1 (8 ounce) carton frozen whipped topping, thawed	227 g
3 tablespoons semi-sweet chocolate, melted	45 ml

- Preheat oven to 350° (176° C).
- Lightly grease bottom of 9 x 13-inch (23 x 33 cm) baking pan. Press brownie dough evenly into pan.
- Bake for 20 minutes. Remove from oven and cool.
- In large bowl, beat cream cheese and sugar until they mix well.
- Add whipped topping and beat on low speed.
- Remove one-third of cream cheese mixture and set aside. Stir chocolate into remaining two-thirds of mixture.
- Spread chocolate-cheese mixture evenly over cooled brownie crust. Carefully spread plain cream cheese mixture over top.
- Chill until firm.

Optional: For an extra special touch, drizzle chocolate topping over each slice or grate some chocolate and arrange shavings on surface.

Crunchy Caramel-Topped Cheesecake

This is a terrific 5-minute recipe!

1 (12 ounce) jar caramel ice cream topping or caramel sauce	340 g
1 (6 or 8 inch) prepared cheesecake	20 cm
3 (1.4 ounce) chocolate-covered toffee bars, crushed	3 (43 g)

+ Spread caramel topping over top of cheesecake. Sprinkle crushed toffee over caramel.
+ Cut and serve.

Tip: There's a great caramel sauce recipe on page 263.

Emergency Cheesecake

1 (8 ounce) package cream cheese, softened	227 g
1 (14 ounce) can sweetened condensed milk	396 g
½ cup lemon juice	120 ml
1 teaspoon vanilla extract	5 ml
1 (9 inch) prepared graham cracker piecrust	23 cm

+ Blend cream cheese, condensed milk, lemon juice and vanilla with mixer.
+ Pour mixture into piecrust and refrigerate.

Tip: To serve, top with cherry pie filling.

Strawberry-Topped Cheesecake

Here is a quick way to turn a plain dessert into a sophisticated taste treat in 5 minutes! Take a prepared cheesecake, top it with glazed fresh fruit and serve it with a spiked sauce. You will have an impressive, delicious dessert in no time.

1 pint fresh strawberries	**.5 kg**
1 (8 or 10 inch) prepared plain cheesecake	**1 (25 cm)**
½ cup strawberry preserves	**120 ml**
1 tablespoon raspberry liqueur	**15 ml**

+ Hull strawberries and cut in half. Arrange attractively on top of cheesecake.
+ Warm strawberry preserves in saucepan or microwave for 30 to 45 seconds on HIGH.
+ Stir and brush glaze onto strawberries with a pastry brush.
+ To make sauce, add raspberry liqueur to remaining strawberry preserves and stir well. Serve sauce over slices of cheesecake.

> *Tip: Be sure to serve this right away because the strawberry juice will discolor the cheesecake.*

Cookies
&
Bars

Peanut Butter Cookies

This cookie is fast, inexpensive and good and uses ingredients you usually have on-hand.

1 cup crunchy or smooth peanut butter	**240 ml**
1 cup sugar	**240 ml**
1 egg	
1 teaspoon vanilla extract	**5 ml**

- Preheat oven to 350° (176° C).
- In medium bowl, combine peanut butter with sugar and mix well. Beat in egg and vanilla.
- Roll heaping teaspoonfuls of dough into balls about 1½ inches (3.5 cm) in diameter. Flatten with fork dipped in sugar and criss-crossed. Place 2 inches (5 cm) apart on ungreased baking sheet.
- Bake for 15 minutes.
- Remove from oven and cool cookies on baking sheet for 1 minute before transferring to cooling rack. Yield: 2 dozen cookies.

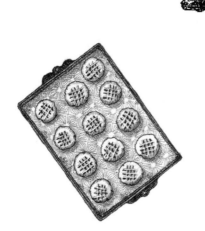

Peanut Butter Chip Cookies

1 (18 ounce) package prepared sugar cookie dough	510 g
½ cup creamy peanut butter	120 ml
½ cup miniature chocolate chips	120 ml
½ cup peanut butter chips	120 ml
½ cup chopped peanuts	120 ml

+ Preheat oven to 350° (176° C).
+ Beat cookie dough and peanut butter in large bowl until they blend and are smooth.
+ Stir in chocolate chips, peanut butter chips and peanuts.
+ Drop dough by heaping tablespoonfuls onto ungreased baking sheet.
+ Bake for 15 minutes.

Peanut Butter-Date Cookies

1 egg, beaten	
⅔ cup sugar	160 ml
⅓ cup packed brown sugar	80 ml
1 cup chunky peanut butter	240 ml
½ cup chopped dates	120 ml

+ Preheat oven to 350° (176° C).
+ Blend egg, sugars and peanut butter and mix thoroughly. Stir in dates and roll into 1-inch (2.5 cm) balls.
+ Place on ungreased cookie sheet and use fork to press each ball down to about ½ inch (1.2 cm).
+ Bake for about 12 minutes and cool before storing.

Easy Peanut Butter Cookies

1⅔ cups powdered sugar	400 ml
1 cup crunchy peanut butter	240 ml
1 large egg	
1 teaspoon vanilla extract	5 ml

- Preheat oven to 325° (162° C).
- In bowl, combine all ingredients and mix well.
- Roll dough into 1-inch (2.5 cm) balls and place on greased baking sheet. Lightly criss-cross cookies with fork.
- Bake 10 minutes and cool several minutes before storing.

Brown Sugar Cookies

1 cup (2 sticks) butter, softened	240 ml
¾ cup packed dark brown sugar	180 ml
1 egg yolk	
1 tablespoon vanilla extract	15 ml
1¼ cups flour	300 ml

- In mixing bowl, beat butter and gradually add brown sugar. Add egg yolk and vanilla and beat well.
- Slowly add flour and dash of salt and mix well.
- Shape dough in 1-inch (2.5 cm) balls and chill 2 hours.
- Place cookie dough on baking sheet and flatten each cookie with back of spoon.
- Bake at 350° (176° C) for 10 to 12 minutes.

Oatmeal-Chocolate Chip Cookies

1 (18 ounce) box yellow cake mix	510 g
1 cup quick-cook rolled oats	240 ml
¾ cup (1½ sticks) butter, softened	180 ml
2 eggs	
1 cup semi-sweet chocolate chips	240 ml

+ Preheat oven to 350° (176° C).
+ In large bowl, combine cake mix, oats, butter and eggs and beat until they blend well.
+ Stir in chocolate chips.
+ Drop by teaspoonfuls onto ungreased baking sheet.
+ Bake 10 to 12 minutes or until light brown.
+ Allow cookies to cool slightly, remove from baking sheet and cool completely on wire rack.

Coconut-Chocolate Drops

1 cup sweetened condensed milk	240 ml
4 cups flaked coconut	1.1 L
⅔ cup miniature semi-sweet chocolate bits	160 ml
1 teaspoon vanilla extract	5 ml
½ teaspoon almond extract	2 ml

+ Stir condensed milk and coconut together to form a gooey mixture.
+ Add chocolate bits, vanilla and almond extracts and stir until they blend well.
+ Drop by teaspoonfuls onto sprayed baking sheet.
+ Bake at 325° (162° C) for 12 minutes.

Coconut Moments

1 cup (2 sticks) butter, softened	240 ml
½ cup powdered sugar	120 ml
½ cup cornstarch	120 ml
1⅓ cups flour	320 ml
Flaked coconut	

- Beat butter and powdered sugar until light and fluffy. Add cornstarch and flour; beat until they blend well. Cover and refrigerate for 1 hour.
- Remove and shape into 1-inch (2.5 cm) balls. Roll balls in flaked coconut and place on ungreased baking sheet.
- Bake at 325° (162° C) for 12 to 15 minutes. Watch closely and do not let coconut burn.
- Cool 2 to 3 minutes before removing from pan.

Kiss Me Chocolate

2 egg whites	
⅔ cup sugar	160 ml
1 teaspoon vanilla extract	5 ml
1¼ cups chopped pecans	300 ml
1 (6 ounce) package chocolate chips	168 g

- Preheat oven to 375° (190° C).
- Beat egg whites until very stiff. Blend in sugar, vanilla and dash of salt.
- Fold in pecans and chocolate chips.
- Drop dough by teaspoonfuls onto shiny side of foil on baking sheet.
- Put cookies in oven, TURN OVEN OFF and leave overnight. (If cookies are a little sticky the next morning, leave out in air to dry.)

Chocolate-Cherry Cookies

1 (18 ounce) box cherry cake mix	510 g
¾ cup (1½ sticks) butter, softened	180 ml
2 eggs	
1 cup miniature semi-sweet chocolate chips	240 ml

- Preheat oven to 350° (176° C).
- In large bowl, combine cake mix, butter and eggs and mix well. Stir in chocolate chips.
- Drop dough by rounded teaspoonfuls onto greased baking sheet.
- Bake 10 to 12 minutes.
- Cool slightly on baking sheet and move to cooling rack. Drizzle cookies with glaze.

Glaze:

1 cup miniature semi-sweet chocolate chips	240 ml
3 tablespoons shortening	45 ml

- Place both ingredients in microwave-safe bowl, microwave on HIGH for 45 seconds and stir. (If chocolate melts and mixture is smooth, pour over cookies; if not, microwave another 15 to 20 seconds.)

Cheesecake Cookies

1 cup (2 sticks) butter, softened	240 ml
2 (3 ounce) packages cream cheese, softened	2 (84 g)
2 cups sugar	480 ml
2 cups flour	480 ml

+ Cream butter, cream cheese and sugar and beat well.
+ Add flour and mix well.
+ Drop by teaspoonfuls onto cookie sheet and bake at 350° (176° C) for 12 to 15 minutes or until edges are golden brown.

Tip: These are made even better by adding 1 cup (240 ml) chopped pecans.

Old-Fashioned Peach Cookies

1 (20 ounce) can peach pie filling	567 g
1 (18 ounce) box yellow cake mix	510 g
2 eggs	
1 cup finely chopped pecans	240 ml
Sugar	

+ In blender, process pie filling until smooth.
+ In large bowl, combine pie filling, dry cake mix and eggs and blend well.
+ Stir in pecans.
+ Drop by tablespoonfuls onto greased baking sheet.
+ Sprinkle with sugar.
+ Bake at 350° (176° C) for 15 minutes or until cookies are light brown around edges.

110

Orange-Pecan Cookies

*The cake mix makes these cookies a breeze
because you have a head start.*

2 cups pecan halves, divided	480 ml
1 (18 ounce) box orange cake mix	510 g
1 (8 ounce) carton vanilla yogurt	227 g
1 egg	
2 tablespoons (¼ stick) butter	30 ml

+ Preheat oven to 350° (176° C).
+ Chop 1 cup pecans and set aside.
+ In large bowl, combine dry cake mix with yogurt, egg and butter. Beat on low speed just until they blend.
+ Stir in chopped pecans
+ Drop by rounded teaspoonfuls onto greased baking sheet and press whole pecan half on top of each cookie.
+ Bake 11 to 13 minutes or until light brown.
+ Remove from oven, cool cookies for 1 minute and transfer to cooling rack.

Butter Pecan Cookies

1 cup (2 sticks) butter, softened	240 ml
½ cup firmly packed light brown sugar	120 ml
1 large egg	
2 cups flour	480 ml
¾ cup chopped pecans, toasted	180 ml

- In medium bowl, beat butter and sugar until light and fluffy. Beat in egg.
- Add flour and beat until they blend well. Stir in pecans.
- Divide dough in half. Shape each half into 8 x 1½-inch (20 x 3.5 cm) logs.
- Cover each log well in wax paper or plastic wrap and freeze until firm, about 30 minutes, or chill for up to 2 days.
- When ready to bake, preheat oven to 350° (176° C).
- Slice dough into pieces ⅓-inch (.8 cm) thick and place slices 2 inches (5 cm) apart on ungreased baking sheet.
- Bake for 15 minutes or until cookies are light brown around edges. Remove from oven and transfer cookies to cooling rack.

Pecan Puffs

2 egg whites	
¾ cup packed light brown sugar	180 ml
1 teaspoon vanilla extract	5 ml
1 cup chopped pecans	240 ml

+ Preheat oven to 250° (121° C).
+ Beat egg whites until foamy and add brown sugar, ¼ cup (60 ml) at a time.
+ Add vanilla, continue beating until stiff peaks form (about 3 or 4 minutes) and fold in pecans.
+ Line cookie sheet with parchment paper and drop mixture by teaspoonfuls onto paper.
+ Bake for 45 minutes.

Butter Pecan Dreams

1 cup (2 sticks) butter, softened	240 ml
½ cup sugar	120 ml
2 teaspoons vanilla extract	10 ml
2 cups flour	480 ml
2 cups chopped pecans	480 ml

+ Preheat oven to 300° (148° C).
+ Cream butter and sugar and add vanilla.
+ Stir in flour and chopped pecans.
+ Roll dough into small balls and place on ungreased baking sheet.
+ Bake 30 to 45 minutes.
+ Remove from oven and roll in granulated or powdered sugar.

Yummy Cookies

3 egg whites	
1¼ cups sugar	300 ml
2 teaspoons vanilla extract	10 ml
3½ cups frosted corn flakes	830 ml
1 cup chopped pecans	240 ml

+ Preheat oven to 250° (121° C).
+ Beat egg whites until stiff and gradually add sugar and vanilla.
+ Fold in frosted corn flakes and pecans and drop by teaspoonfuls on cookie sheet lined with parchment paper.
+ Bake for 40 minutes.

Almond-Meringue Cookies

2 egg whites	
½ cup sugar	120 ml
⅛ teaspoon almond extract	.5 ml

+ Preheat oven to 250° (121° C).
+ Line baking sheet with parchment paper or aluminum foil and set aside.
+ In medium bowl, beat egg whites on high speed until soft peaks form.
+ Gradually add sugar, beating after each addition, until mixture is glossy and holds stiff peaks.
+ Mix in almond extract on low speed.
+ Drop dough by rounded teaspoonfuls onto baking sheet about 1 inch (2.5 cm) apart.
+ Bake for 1 hour. Turn oven off and leave cookies in oven for another 2 hours.
+ Remove from paper or foil and store in airtight container.

Amaretti

These are light, little Italian cookies with a crispy, melt-in-your-mouth outside and a soft, chewy inside.

2 egg whites
Pinch salt
1 cup sugar   240 ml
1 teaspoon almond extract   5 ml
1 cup finely ground almonds   240 ml

+ Preheat oven to 300° (148° C).
+ In medium bowl, beat egg whites with mixer until frothy and add salt. Add sugar gradually, about   1 tablespoon (15 ml) at a time, while beating on high speed until stiff peaks form.
+ Fold in almond extract and almonds and drop dough by rounded teaspoonfuls onto parchment paper-lined baking sheets.
+ Bake for 25 to 30 minutes or until cookies are very light brown.
+ Remove from oven and cool cookies. Peel cookies from paper and store in airtight container. Yield: 2 to 2½ dozen cookies.

Ladyfingers

3 eggs, separated
1 teaspoon almond extract   **5 ml**
⅓ cup sugar   **80 ml**
½ cup cake flour   **120 ml**
1 teaspoon baking powder   **5 ml**

- Beat egg yolks until thick and lemon colored. Beat in almond extract.
- In separate bowl, beat egg whites until stiff peaks form. Continue beating and gradually add sugar until mixture is glossy and stiff.
- Fold egg yolk mixture into egg white mixture.
- Sift flour and baking powder together and gently fold into egg mixture.
- Fill pastry bag and pipe mixture onto ungreased baking sheet in 3-inch (8 cm) lengths about 1 inch (2.5 cm) wide.
- Bake 10 minutes. Remove from baking sheet and cool.

Mexican Wedding Cookies

1 cup (2 sticks) butter, softened	240 ml
1 cup powdered sugar, divided	240 ml
½ teaspoon vanilla extract	2 ml
1¾ cups flour	420 ml
½ cup chopped pecans or walnuts	120 ml

+ Cream butter and ¾ cup (180 ml) powdered sugar. Beat in vanilla, flour and nuts.
+ Cover and chill dough for about 1 hour.
+ When ready to bake, preheat oven to 350° (176° C).
+ Shape dough into 1-inch (2.5 cm) balls and place 2 inches (2.5 cm) apart on ungreased baking sheet.
+ Bake for 20 minutes.
+ Remove from oven and transfer to cooling rack. When cool, roll in remaining ¼ cup (60 ml) powdered sugar.

Easy Sand Tarts

1 cup (2 sticks) butter, softened	240 ml
¾ cup powdered sugar	180 ml
2 cups sifted flour	480 ml
1 cup chopped pecans	240 ml
1 teaspoon vanilla extract	5 ml

+ Preheat oven to 325° (162° C).
+ In mixing bowl, cream butter and powdered sugar. Slowly add flour, pecans and vanilla.
+ Roll into crescents and place on ungreased baking sheet.
+ Bake for 20 minutes.
+ Roll in extra powdered sugar after tarts cool.

Snappy Almond-Sugar Cookies

1 cup (2 sticks) butter, softened	240 ml
1 cup plus 2 tablespoons sugar, divided	240 ml
½ teaspoon almond extract	2 ml
2 cups flour	480 ml
1 cup chopped almonds	240 ml

- Cream butter, 1 cup (240 ml) sugar and almond extract until light and fluffy. Slowly beat in flour and stir in almonds.
- Shape dough into roll, wrap and chill well, about 2 hours.
- Preheat oven to 325° (148° C).
- Slice roll into ¼-inch (.6 cm) pieces and bake for 20 minutes.
- Sprinkle with remaining 2 tablespoons (30 ml) sugar while still hot.

Gingerbread Cookies

¾ cup (1½ sticks) butter, softened	180 ml
2 egg yolks	
1 (18 ounce) box spice cake mix	510 g
1 teaspoon ginger	5 ml

- In large bowl, combine butter and egg yolks. Gradually add cake mix and ginger and blend well.
- Roll dough to ⅛-inch (.3 cm) thickness on lightly floured surface. Using gingerbread cookie cutter, cut out cookies and place 2 inches (5 cm) apart on baking sheet.
- Bake at 375° (190° C) for about 8 minutes or until edges are slightly brown. Cool before transferring cookies to a cookie jar.

Disappearing Cookies

1 (18 ounce) box butter cake mix	510 g
1 (3.4 ounce) package instant butterscotch pudding mix	98 g
1 cup oil	240 ml
1 egg, beaten	1
1¼ cups chopped pecans	300 ml

+ By hand, stir together cake mix and pudding mix and slowly add oil.
+ Add egg and mix thoroughly. Stir in pecans.
+ Drop cookie dough by teaspoonfuls about 2 inches (5 cm) apart on baking sheet.
+ Bake at 350° (176° C) for 8 to 9 minutes. (Do not overbake.)

Butter Cookies

1 pound butter, softened	.5 kg
¾ cup packed brown sugar	180 ml
¾ cup sugar	180 ml
4½ cups flour	1.2 ml

+ Cream butter and both sugars, slowly add flour and mix well. (Dough will be very thick.)
+ Roll dough into small balls and place on ungreased baking sheet.
+ Bake at 350° (176° C) for about 15 minutes until light brown. Do not overbake.

Easy Sugar Cookies

1 (8 ounce) package cream cheese, softened	227 g
¾ cup sugar	180 ml
1 cup (2 sticks) butter, softened	240 ml
½ teaspoon lemon extract	2 ml
2½ cups flour	600 ml

+ In medium bowl, combine cream cheese, sugar, butter and lemon extract. Beat until ingredients blend well.
+ Add flour and mix thoroughly. Cover and chill several hours or overnight.
+ When ready to bake, preheat oven to 375° (190° C) and roll dough out on lightly floured surface to ⅛-inch (.3 cm) thickness.
+ Cut shapes with cookie cutter and place on ungreased baking sheet.
+ Bake 6 to 8 minutes. Remove from oven, cool cookies for 1 minute on baking sheet and transfer to cooling rack.

Optional: Before baking, lightly brush cookies with beaten egg and sprinkle with colored sugar or candy.

Charlie McRoons

We used to call these Chocolate Macaroons, but a
sweet little 3-year-old renamed them for us.

2 egg whites	
1 (4 ounce) package sweet baking chocolate	**114 g**
½ cup sugar	**120 ml**
¼ teaspoon vanilla extract	**1 ml**
1 (7 ounce) package flaked coconut	**98 g**

+ Divide egg whites and allow to reach room temperature.
+ Place chocolate in top of double boiler. Stir occasionally until chocolate melts and remove from heat to cool.
+ Beat egg whites at high speed for 1 minute. Gradually add sugar, 1 tablespoon (15 ml) at a time and beat until stiff peaks form, about 3 minutes.
+ Add chocolate and vanilla, beat well and stir in coconut.
+ Drop by teaspoonfuls onto baking sheet lined with parchment paper.
+ Bake at 350° (176° C) for 12 to 15 minutes. Transfer paper to wire rack and cool cookies completely.

Fast Chocolate Macaroons

These are really fast, delicious cookies.

4 (1 ounce) squares unsweetened baking chocolate, melted	4(28 g)
1 (14 ounce) can sweetened condensed milk	396 g
2 teaspoons vanilla extract	10 ml
1 (14 ounce) package flaked coconut	396 g

+ Preheat oven to 350° (176° C).
+ In large bowl, combine chocolate, sweetened condensed milk and vanilla. Stir until they blend well and mixture is evenly colored. Stir in coconut.
+ Drop dough by heaping teaspoonfuls onto greased baking sheet about 2 inches (5 cm) apart.
+ Bake for 10 minutes.
+ Remove from oven and immediately transfer to cooling rack. Yield: 3½ dozen cookies.

Coconut Bites

1 (12 ounce) package white chocolate baking chips	340 g
¼ cup (½ stick) butter	60 ml
16 large marshmallows	
2 cups quick-cooking oats	480 ml
1 cup flaked coconut	240 ml

+ In saucepan over low heat, melt chocolate chips, butter and marshmallows and stir until smooth.
+ Stir in oats and coconut and mix well.
+ Drop by rounded teaspoonfuls onto wax paper-lined baking sheets.
+ Chill until set.

Macaroons

2 large egg whites	
3 tablespoons sugar	45 ml
½ teaspoon vanilla extract	2 ml
½ teaspoon almond extract	2 ml
½ cup sweetened, flaked coconut	120 ml

+ Preheat oven to 300° (148° C).
+ Line large baking sheet with foil, prepare foil with non-stick spray and lightly dust with flour (shake off excess flour).
+ In bowl, whisk egg whites, sugar, extracts and a pinch of salt. Stir in coconut.
+ Drop heaping tablespoons of mixture on prepared baking sheet about 2 inches (5 cm) apart.
+ Bake about 18 minutes or until tops are light brown in spots.
+ Carefully transfer foil with cookies from baking sheet to wire rack and cool completely. Peel macaroons from foil.

Potato Chip Crunchies

1 cup (2 sticks) butter, softened	240 ml
⅔ cup sugar	160 ml
1 teaspoon vanilla extract	5 ml
1½ cups flour	360 ml
½ cup crushed potato chips	120 ml

+ Cream butter, sugar and vanilla and stir in flour.
+ Carefully fold in potato chips.
+ Drop by teaspoonfuls on ungreased baking sheet.
+ Bake at 350° (176° C) for about 12 minutes or until light brown.

Butterscotch Haystacks

1 (6 ounce) package chocolate chips	168 g
1 (6 ounce) package butterscotch chips	168 g
1 cup salted peanuts	240 ml
1 (5 ounce) can chow mein noodles	143 g

+ In large saucepan, melt chocolate and butterscotch chips.
+ Add peanuts and noodles and mix well.
+ Drop by teaspoonfuls onto wax paper and chill to harden.

No-Bake Chocolate Drops

1 (6 ounce) package semi-sweet chocolate baking chips	168 g
½ cup crunchy peanut butter	120 ml
1 (5 ounce) package chow mein noodles	143 ml
1 cup salted, roasted peanuts	240 ml

+ In saucepan, combine baking chips and peanut butter and heat on low. Stir constantly until chocolate melts.
+ Add noodles and peanuts and stir until ingredients coat evenly with chocolate.
+ Drop by heaping teaspoonfuls onto wax paper and chill.

Corn Flake Cookies

1 (12 ounce) package butterscotch morsels	340 g
¾ cup peanut butter	180 ml
3½ to 4 cups corn flakes, crushed	1.1 L

+ Melt butterscotch morsels on very low heat and add peanut butter.
+ When mixed thoroughly, add corn flakes.
+ Drop by teaspoonfuls onto wax paper.

Tumbleweeds

1 (12 ounce) can salted peanuts	340 g
1 (7 ounce) can potato sticks, broken up	198 g
3 cups butterscotch chips	710 ml
3 tablespoons peanut butter	45 ml

+ Combine peanuts and potato sticks in bowl and set aside.
+ In microwave, heat butterscotch chips and peanut butter at 70% power for 1 to 2 minutes (or until they melt) and stir every 30 seconds.
+ Add to peanut-potato stick mixture and stir to coat evenly.
+ Drop by rounded tablespoonfuls onto wax paper-lined baking sheet.
+ Refrigerate until set, about 10 minutes.

Scotch Crunchies

½ cup crunchy peanut butter	120 ml
1 (6 ounce) package butterscotch bits	168 g
2½ cups frosted flakes	600 ml
½ cup peanuts	120 ml

+ Combine peanut butter and butterscotch bits in large saucepan and melt over low heat.
+ Stir until butterscotch bits melt and stir in cereal and peanuts.
+ Drop by teaspoonfuls onto wax paper.
+ Refrigerate until firm and store in airtight container.

Peanut Butter Crunchies

1 cup sugar	240 ml
¾ cup light corn syrup	180 ml
1 (16 ounce) jar crunchy peanut butter	.5 kg
4½ cups chow mein noodles	1.2 L

+ In saucepan over medium heat, bring sugar and corn syrup to boil and stir in peanut butter.
+ Remove from heat and stir in noodles.
+ Drop by spoonfuls onto wax paper and allow to cool.

Peanut Butter Balls

¾ cup light corn syrup	180 ml
2½ cups crunchy peanut butter	600 ml
2¼ cups graham cracker crumbs	540 ml
1¼ cups powdered sugar	300 ml

+ In bowl, combine all ingredients and mix until smooth.
+ Shape dough into 1-inch (2.5 cm) balls and place on wax paper-lined baking sheet. Chill for about 30 minutes.

If you would like to make this for a kids' party, pour some chocolate syrup or ice cream topping in a shallow bowl and let the kids dip their Peanut Butter Balls in chocolate. (Of course, it might get messy, so have the paper towels ready.)

Peanut Krispies

¾ cup (1½ sticks) butter	180 ml
2 cups peanut butter	480 ml
1 (16 ounce) box powdered sugar	.5 kg
3½ cups crispy rice cereal	830 ml
¾ cup chopped peanuts	180 ml

+ Melt butter in large saucepan, add peanut butter and mix well.
+ Add powdered sugar, crispy rice cereal and peanuts and mix.
+ Drop by teaspoonfuls onto wax paper.

127

Peanutty Chocolate Tortillas

4 (8 inch) flour tortillas	**4(20 cm)**
¼ cup peanut butter, divided	**60 ml**
¼ cup marshmallow cream, divided	**60 ml**
2 bananas, sliced, divided	
½ cup milk chocolate chips, divided	**120 ml**

- Lightly coat 1 side of each tortilla with cooking spray. Place tortillas on work surface, sprayed side down.
- Spread 1 tablespoon (15 ml) peanut butter over half of each tortilla. Spread 1 tablespoon (15 cm) marshmallow cream over other half of each tortilla.
- Place ¼ banana slices and 2 tablespoons (30 ml) chocolate chips over marshmallow cream and fold tortilla over to cover filling.
- Heat large, non-stick skillet over medium heat.
- Place each tortilla in skillet for 1 to 2 minutes or until golden brown and crispy.
- Cool slightly and serve.

Caramel Treats

24 chocolate graham cracker squares
1 cup (2 sticks) butter   240 ml
1 cup firmly packed brown sugar   240 ml
1½ cups chopped pecans   360 ml

+ Preheat oven to 350° (176° C).
+ Place single layer of graham cracker squares (do not separate) in bottom of greased jelly-roll pan or on baking sheet with rim.
+ In medium saucepan, combine butter and brown sugar and bring to boil. Simmer for 2 minutes or until mixture starts to thicken. Stir constantly.
+ Remove butter mixture from heat and immediately pour evenly over graham crackers.
+ Sprinkle pecans evenly over top.
+ Bake for 15 minutes. Remove from oven and cool.

Kids' Delight

¼ cup (½ stick) butter   60 ml
1 (10 ounce) package marshmallows   280 g
6 cups cocoa-flavored crispy rice cereal   1.5 L
½ cup miniature chocolate chips   120 ml

+ Spray 9 x 13-inch (23 x 33 cm) baking pan with non-stick spray.
+ In large saucepan over low heat, melt butter and add marshmallows. Stir constantly until marshmallows melt and remove from heat.
+ Stir in cereal and chocolate chips. Spoon into prepared pan and use spatula to level cereal mixture.
+ When cool, cut into squares.

Butterscotch Sweets

½ cup butterscotch chips	120 ml
¼ cup flaked coconut	60 ml
2 tablespoons chopped nuts	30 ml
1 (8 ounce) can crescent dinner rolls	227 g
Powdered sugar	

- Preheat oven to 375° (190° C).
- In small bowl, mix butterscotch chips, coconut and nuts.
- Unroll crescent roll dough to form 8 triangles.
- Sprinkle 1 heaping tablespoon (15 cm) butterscotch mixture on top of each dough triangle and roll each triangle into jellyroll.
- Place rolls, seam side down, on ungreased baking sheet.
- Bake 10 to 12 minutes or until golden brown.
- Sprinkle with powdered sugar.

Nutty Orange Logs

1 (12 ounce) box vanilla wafers, crushed	340 g
½ cup (1 stick) butter, melted	120 ml
1 (16 ounce) box powdered sugar	.5 kg
1 (6 ounce) can frozen orange juice concentrate	168 g
1 cup finely chopped pecans	240 ml

- Combine wafers, butter, sugar and juice concentrate and mix well.
- Form mixture into balls and roll in chopped pecans. Store in airtight container.

Crispy Fudge Treats

6 cups crispy rice cereal	1.5 L
¾ cup powdered sugar	180 ml
1¾ cups semi-sweet chocolate chips	420 ml
½ cup light corn syrup	120 ml
⅓ cup (⅔ stick) butter	80 ml

+ Combine cereal and powdered sugar in large bowl and set aside.
+ Place chocolate chips, corn syrup and butter in 1-quart (1 L) microwave-safe dish.
+ Microwave, uncovered, on HIGH for about 1 minute and stir until smooth. (If you have vanilla extract on hand, stir in 2 teaspoons (10 ml) vanilla.)
+ Pour chocolate mixture over cereal mixture and mix well.
+ Spoon into greased 9 x 13-inch (23 x 33 cm) pan, refrigerate for 30 minutes and cut into squares.

Crazy Cocoa Crisps

24 ounces white almond bark	680 g
2¼ cups cocoa-flavored crispy rice cereal	540 ml
2 cups dry-roasted peanuts	480 ml

· Place almond bark in top of double boiler. Heat and stir while bark melts.
· Stir in cereal and peanuts.
· Drop by teaspoonfuls onto baking sheet.
· Refrigerate for 30 minutes to set. Store in airtight container.

Sweet Memories

¾ cup whipping cream	180 ml
1 (12 ounce) package milk chocolate chips	340 g
4 cups miniature marshmallows	1.1 L
1 (7.5 ounce) package	
chocolate-covered graham crackers	210 g

+ Place whipping cream in large saucepan over medium-low heat.
+ Add chocolate chips and stir until they melt.
+ Remove from heat. Add marshmallows and stir to coat.
+ Break graham crackers into bite-size pieces (do not crush) and gently stir into cream-marshmallow mixture.
+ Spread into foil-covered 9-inch (23 cm) square pan. Refrigerate at least 3 hours or until firm.
+ Cut into squares to serve.

Morning Meringues

2 egg whites	
¾ cup sugar	180 ml
1 cup chopped nuts	240 ml
1 cup chocolate chips	240 ml

+ Beat egg whites until stiff and add sugar.
+ Fold in nuts and chocolate chips.
+ Line baking sheet with aluminum foil, drop dough by teaspoonfuls onto foil and press down.
+ Bake at 350° ((176° C) for 10 minutes. Turn oven off and let cookies sit in oven for 8 to 10 hours.

Crispy Peanut Butter Bars

This is a quick, tasty treat great for taking to functions or a bake sale. The bars stay crispy and are fairly neat to eat and easy to wrap.

3 tablespoons butter	**45 ml**
4 cups miniature marshmallows	**1.1 L**
½ cup peanut butter	**120 ml**
6 cups crispy rice cereal	**1.5 L**

+ Melt butter in medium saucepan over low heat.
+ Add marshmallows and stir until they melt. Remove from heat.
+ Stir peanut butter into marshmallow mixture until smooth.
+ Add cereal and quickly stir until mixture coats cereal.
+ Press mixture into buttered 9 x 13-inch (23 x 33 cm) baking pan and cool. Cut into bars.

Optional: Consider chocolate-covered bars. Melt 2 cups (480 ml) semi-sweet or milk chocolate chips and spread chocolate over bars. Let set, cut and serve.

Everyday Special Brownies

1 cup (2 sticks) butter	240 ml
1½ cups dark chocolate pieces	360 ml
3 eggs	
1¼ cups sugar	300 ml
1 cup flour	240 ml

+ Preheat oven to 350° (176° C).
+ Melt butter and chocolate in double boiler over low heat. Cool to room temperature.
+ In medium bowl, beat eggs until foamy. Stir in sugar and beat at medium speed for 2 to 3 minutes.
+ Reduce speed and slowly pour chocolate-butter mixture into egg mixture. Slowly beat in flour in several additions.
+ Pour into greased, floured 9 x 13-inch (23 x 33 cm) baking pan.
+ Bake for 35 to 40 minutes or until brownies are done in middle. Cool and cut into squares.

Easy Blonde Brownies

1 (16 ounce) box light brown sugar	.5 kg
4 eggs	
2 cups biscuit mix	480 ml
2 cups chopped pecans	480 ml

+ Preheat oven to 350° (176° C).
+ In mixing bowl, beat brown sugar, eggs and biscuit mix. Stir in pecans and pour into greased 9 x 13-inch (23 x 33 cm) baking pan.
+ Bake for 35 minutes. Cool and cut into squares.

Snicker Brownies

1 (18 ounce) box German chocolate cake mix	510 g
¾ cup (1½ sticks) butter, melted	180 ml
½ cup evaporated milk	120 ml
4 (2.7 ounce) Snicker candy bars,	4 (78 g)
cut in ⅛-inch slices	.3 cm

+ Preheat oven to 350° (176° C).
+ In large bowl, combine cake mix, butter and evaporated milk and beat on low speed until mixture blends well.
+ Place half batter in greased, floured 9 x 13-inch (23 x 33 cm) baking pan and bake for 10 minutes. Remove from oven and place candy bar slices evenly over brownies.
+ Drop remaining half of batter by spoonfuls over candy bars and spread as evenly as possible.
+ Place back in oven and bake for 20 minutes longer. When cool, cut into bars.

Chocolate Chip-Cheese Bars

1 (18 ounce) tube refrigerated chocolate chip cookie dough, divided	510 g
1 (8 ounce) package cream cheese, softened	227 g
½ cup sugar	120 ml
1 egg	

+ Cut cookie dough in half and press half of dough into bottom of greased 9-inch square (23 cm) or 7 x 11-inch (18 x 28 cm) baking pan.
+ In mixing bowl, beat cream cheese, sugar and egg until smooth. Spread over pressed cookie dough and sprinkle remaining dough over top.
+ Bake at 350° (176° C) for 35 to 40 minutes or until toothpick inserted near center comes out clean.
+ Cool on wire rack and cut into bars. Refrigerate leftovers.

Coconut-Brownie Bars

2 (18 ounce) tubes chocolate chip cookie dough	2 (340 g)
2 eggs	
⅓ cup oil	80 ml
1 (18 ounce) box brownie mix	340 g
1 cup chopped walnuts	240 ml
1 cup flaked coconut	240 ml

+ Preheat oven to 350° (176° C).
+ Spray 10 x 15-inch (25 x 38 cm) jellyroll pan with non-stick spray and press cookie dough into bottom of pan.
+ In large bowl, combine eggs, oil, brownie mix and ¼ cup (60 ml) water and mix until they blend well.
+ Spoon brownie mixture over cookie dough and sprinkle with walnuts and coconut.
+ Bake for 1 hour. Cool before slicing into bars.

Walnut Bars

1⅔ cups graham cracker crumbs	400 ml
1½ cups coarsely chopped walnuts	360 ml
1 (14 ounce) can sweetened condensed milk	396 g
¼ cup flaked coconut, optional	60 ml

+ Place cracker crumbs and walnuts in bowl. Slowly add sweetened condensed milk, coconut and pinch of salt. (Mixture will be very thick.)
+ Pack mixture into greased 9-inch (23 cm) square pan with back of spoon.
+ Bake at 350° (176° C) for 35 minutes. When cool, cut into squares.

German Chocolate Brownie Bars

1 (14 ounce) package caramels, unwrapped	396 g
1 (12 ounce) can evaporated milk, divided	340 g
1 (18 ounce) box chocolate cake mix	510 g
1 cup chopped pecans	240 ml
1 cup semi-sweet chocolate chips	240 ml

+ Preheat oven to 350° (176° C).
+ Combine caramels with ⅓ cup (80 ml) evaporated milk in top of double boiler over simmering water.
+ Stir until caramels melt and mixture is smooth. Remove from heat and set aside.
+ In large bowl, combine cake mix with pecans and remaining evaporated milk.
+ Spread half of batter in bottom of greased 9 x 13-inch (23 x 33 cm) baking pan.
+ Bake for 6 minutes. Remove from oven, sprinkle with chocolate chips and drizzle caramel mixture evenly over top.
+ Drop remaining half of batter by spoonfuls over caramel mixture.
+ Bake another 15 to 20 minutes. Remove from oven and cool before cutting.

Rocky Road Bars

1 (12 ounce) package semi-sweet chocolate morsels	340 g
1 (14 ounce) can sweetened condensed milk	396 g
2 tablespoons (¼ stick) butter	30 ml
2 cups dry-roasted peanuts	480 ml
1 (10 ounce) package miniature marshmallows	280 g

+ Place chocolate morsels, sweetened condensed milk and butter in double boiler and heat on low. Stir constantly until chocolate melts.
+ Remove from heat and stir in peanuts and marshmallows.
+ Quickly spread mixture onto wax paper-lined 9 x 13-inch (23 x 33 cm) pan. Chill at least 2 hours.
+ Cut into bars and store in refrigerator.

Pecan Squares

1 (24 ounce) package almond bark	680 g
1 cup cinnamon chips	240 ml
1 cup chopped pecans	240 ml
8 cups frosted crispy rice cereal	1.8 L

+ Melt almond bark and cinnamon chips in very large saucepan or roaster over low heat and stir constantly.
+ After they melt, remove from heat and add pecans and cereal.
+ Mix well and stir into 9 x 13-inch (23 x 33 cm) pan. Pat mixture down with back of spoon.
+ Refrigerate just until set and cut into squares.

Caramel-Chocolate Chip Bars

1 (18 ounce) box caramel cake mix	510 g
2 eggs	
⅓ cup firmly packed light brown sugar	80 ml
¼ cup (½ stick) butter, softened	60 ml
1 cup semi-sweet chocolate chips	240 ml

- Combine cake mix, eggs, brown sugar, butter and ¼ cup (60 ml) water in large bowl. Stir until mixture blends thoroughly. (Mixture will be thick.)
- Stir in chocolate chips and spread in greased, floured 9 x 13-inch (23 x 33 cm) baking pan.
- Bake at 350° (176° C) for about 25 to 30 minutes or until toothpick inserted in center comes out clean. Cool before cutting.

Hello Dollies

1½ cups graham cracker crumbs	360 ml
1 (6 ounce) package chocolate chips	168 g
1 cup flaked coconut	240 ml
1¼ cups chopped pecans	300 ml
1 (14 ounce) can sweetened condensed milk	396 g

- Preheat oven to 350° (176° C).
- Sprinkle cracker crumbs in 9 x 9-inch (23 x 33 cm) pan.
- Layer chocolate chips, coconut and pecans and pour sweetened condensed milk over top of layered ingredients.
- Bake for 25 to 30 minutes. Cool and cut into squares.

Chocolate Bars

1 (20 ounce) package chocolate-flavored candy-coating squares	567 g
¾ cup light corn syrup	180 ml
¼ cup (½ stick) butter	60 ml
2 teaspoons vanilla extract	10 ml
8 cups crispy rice cereal	1.8 L

+ Combine chocolate coating, corn syrup and butter in double boiler. Heat on low, stirring occasionally, until coating melts. Remove from heat and stir in vanilla.
+ Place cereal in large mixing bowl, pour chocolate mixture over top and stir until mixture completely coats cereal.
+ Quickly spoon mixture into buttered 9 x 13-inch (23 x 33 cm) baking dish and press down using back of spoon.
+ Cool and cut into bars.

Rainbow Cookie Ribbons

White chocolate bits taste great in this too!

½ cup (1 stick) butter	120 ml
2 cups graham cracker crumbs	480 ml
1 (14 ounce) can sweetened condensed milk	396 g
⅔ cup flaked coconut	160 ml
1 cup chopped pecans	240 ml
1 cup M&Ms plain chocolate candies	240 ml

- Melt butter in oven in 9 x 13-inch (23 x 33 cm) baking pan.
- Sprinkle crumbs over butter and pour sweetened condensed milk over crumbs.
- Top with coconut, pecans and chocolate candies. Press down to even out.
- Bake at 350° (176° C) for 25 to 30 minutes or until light brown. Cool and cut into bars.

Honey-Nut Bars

⅓ cup (⅔ stick) butter	80 ml
¼ cup cocoa	60 ml
1 (10 ounce) package miniature marshmallows	280 g
6 cups honey-nut clusters cereal	1.5 L

- Melt butter in large saucepan and stir in cocoa and marshmallows.
- Cook over low heat, stirring constantly, until marshmallows melt and mixture is smooth.
- Remove from heat and stir in honey-nut clusters.
- Pour into sprayed 7 x 11-inch (18 x 28 cm) pan. With spatula, smooth mixture in pan.
- Cool completely and cut into bars.

Easy Nutty Bars

4 eggs	
1 (16 ounce) box brown sugar	.5 kg
2 tablespoons (¼ stick) butter	30 ml
2 cups self-rising flour	480 ml
1 cup chopped nuts	240 ml

+ Preheat oven to 350° (176° C).
+ Beat eggs and add brown sugar and butter. Place in medium saucepan over low heat and cook until sugar and butter melt.
+ Remove from heat and add flour and nuts.
+ Place in greased 9 x 13-inch (23 x 33 cm) baking pan.
+ Bake for 25 to 30 minutes. Cool and cut into bars.

Toffee Bars

1½ cups (3 sticks) butter, softened	360 ml
1¾ cups packed light brown sugar	420 ml
2 teaspoons vanilla extract	10 ml
3 cups flour	710 ml
1 (8 ounce) package chocolate chips	227 g

+ Preheat oven to 350° (176° C).
+ In mixing bowl, combine butter, brown sugar and vanilla and beat on medium speed for 3 minutes.
+ Add flour, mix until they blend completely and stir in chocolate chips.
+ Place dough on greased 9 x 13-inch (23 x 33 cm) baking pan.
+ Bake 25 minutes or until light brown. Cool slightly and cut into bars.

Easy Gooey Turtle Bars

½ cup (1 stick) butter, melted	120 ml
2 cups vanilla wafer crumbs	480 ml
1 (12 ounce) bag semi-sweet chocolate morsels	340 g
1 cup chopped pecans	240 ml
1 (12 ounce) jar caramel topping	340 g

- Combine butter and wafer crumbs in 9 x 13-inch (23 x 33 cm) baking pan and press into bottom of pan.
- Sprinkle with chocolate morsels and pecans.
- Remove lid from caramel topping and microwave on HIGH for 30 seconds or until hot.
- Drizzle topping over pecans.
- Bake at 350° (176° C) for about 10 to 15 minutes or until morsels melt. (Make sure chocolate morsels melt but crumbs don't burn.)
- Cool in pan and chill at least 30 minutes before cutting into squares.

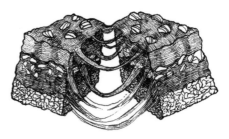

Buttery Walnut Squares

1 cup (2 sticks) butter, softened	240 ml
1¾ cups packed brown sugar	420 ml
1¾ cups flour	420 ml

- Cream butter and brown sugar, add flour and mix well.
- Pat mixture evenly into greased 9 x 13-inch (23 x 33 cm) baking dish.
- Bake at 350° (176° C) for 15 minutes.

Topping:

1 cup packed brown sugar	240 ml
4 eggs, lightly beaten	
2 tablespoons flour	30 ml
2 cups chopped walnuts	480 ml
1 cup flaked coconut	240 ml

- In mixing bowl, combine sugar and eggs. Add flour and mix well.
- Fold in walnuts and coconut and pour over crust.
- Bake at 350° (176° C) for 20 to 25 minutes or just until center is set.
- Cool in pan and cut into squares.

Optional: Top each square with a scoop of vanilla ice cream to serve.

Date-Pecan Bars

Filling:

2 (8 ounce) boxes pitted dates, chopped	2(227 g)
1½ cups orange juice	360 ml
¼ cup sugar	60 ml
¼ teaspoon ground cinnamon	1 ml

Crust and Topping:

1½ cups flour	360 ml
1½ cups oats	360 ml
¾ cup packed brown sugar	180 ml
1½ cups finely chopped pecans	360 ml
1¼ cups (2½ sticks) cold butter, sliced	300 ml

- In saucepan, combine all filling ingredients and bring to boil. Reduce heat, simmer for 15 minutes or until mixture thickens and stir several times.
- Preheat oven to 350° (176° C).
- Place flour, oats, brown sugar and pecans in mixing bowl and cut in butter until mixture is crumbly. Set aside 2½ cups (600 ml) flour mixture for topping.
- Press remaining flour mixture into bottom of greased 9 x 13-inch (23 x 33 cm) baking pan. Spoon filling over crust and spread up to ¼ inch (.6 cm) from edge.
- Sprinkle reserved flour mixture over top of filling.
- Bake for 35 minutes. Cool and cut into bars.

Creamy Pecan Squares

1 (18 ounce) box yellow cake mix	510 g
3 eggs, divided	
½ cup (1 stick) butter, softened	120 ml
2 cups chopped pecans	480 ml
1 (8 ounce) package cream cheese, softened	227 g
3⅔ cups powdered sugar	870 g

- In mixing bowl, combine cake mix, 1 egg and butter. Stir in pecans and mix well.
- Press into greased 9 x 13-inch (23 x 33 cm) baking pan.
- In mixing bowl, beat cream cheese, sugar and remaining 2 eggs until smooth. Pour over pecan mixture.
- Bake at 350° (176° C) for 55 minutes or until golden brown. Cool and cut into squares.

Lemon Cloud Bars

1 (16 ounce) package 1-step angel food cake mix	.5 kg
1 (20 ounce) can lemon pie filling	567 g
⅓ cup (⅔ stick) butter, softened	80 ml
2 cups powdered sugar	480 ml
2 tablespoons lemon juice	30 ml

- Combine cake mix and lemon pie filling and stir until they mix well.
- Pour into greased, floured 9 x 13-inch (23 x 33 cm) baking pan.
- Bake at 350° (176° C) for 25 minutes.
- Just before cake is done, mix butter, powdered sugar and lemon juice and spread over hot cake.
- When cake is cool, cut into bars. Store in refrigerator.

Creamy Strawberry Bars

1 (18 ounce) box strawberry cake mix	510 g
½ cup (1 stick) butter, softened	120 ml
3 eggs, divided	
1 (8 ounce) package cream cheese, softened	227 g
2 cups powdered sugar	480 ml

+ Preheat oven to 325° (162° C).
+ In large bowl, combine cake mix, butter and 1 egg and blend well.
+ Press mixture into bottom of greased 9 x 13-inch (23 x 33 cm) baking dish.
+ In medium bowl, mix cream cheese, 2 eggs and sugar until mixture is smooth. Pour mixture over cake batter.
+ Bake for 30 to 35 minutes or until light brown.

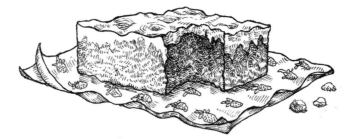

Strawberry Crumbles

2¼ cups biscuit mix	540 ml
1 cup oats	240 ml
1 cup packed brown sugar	240 ml
½ cup (1 stick) butter, softened	120 ml
1 cup strawberry preserves	240 ml

- Preheat oven to 375° (190° C).
- Combine biscuit mix, oats and brown sugar. With pastry blender, cut in butter until mixture is crumbly.
- Press half mixture in bottom of greased 9 x 9-inch (23 x 23 cm) baking pan. Spread strawberry preserves over mixture to within ¼ inch (.6 cm) of edges.
- Sprinkle remaining mixture over top and gently press into preserves.
- Bake 30 minutes or until light brown. Cool and cut into bars to serve.

Puddings
&
Custards

Creamy Banana Pudding

*This is a quick and easy way to make the
old favorite banana pudding.*

1 (14 ounce) can sweetened condensed milk	396 g
1 (3.4 ounce) package instant vanilla pudding mix	98 g
1 (8 ounce) carton whipped topping	227 g
36 vanilla wafers	
3 bananas, peeled, sliced	

+ In large bowl, combine sweetened condensed milk and 1½ cups (360 ml) cold water.
+ Add pudding mix and beat well.
+ Chill 5 minutes then fold in whipped topping.
+ Spoon 1 cup (240 ml) pudding mixture into 3-quart (3 L) glass serving bowl. Top with wafers, banana slices and pudding. Repeat layers twice and end with pudding.
+ Cover and refrigerate.

Crispy-Topped Pudding

2 cups flaked coconut	480 ml
1 cup (2 sticks) butter, melted	240 ml
2 cups flour	480 ml
½ cup sugar	120 ml
2 (22 ounce) containers chocolate or vanilla pudding	2 (624 g)

- Preheat oven to 300° (148° C).
- Combine coconut, butter, flour and sugar and pour into 9 x 13-inch (23 x 33 cm) baking pan. Bake for 45 minutes, stirring every 10 minutes. (Mixture will be crumbly.)
- Remove from oven and set aside half mixture for topping. Spread pudding over crumbs, smooth and sprinkle leftover crumb mixture on top. Chill before serving.

Candy Store Pudding

A special family dessert!

1 cup cold milk	240 ml
1 (4 ounce) package instant chocolate pudding mix	114 g
1 (8 ounce) carton whipped topping	227 g
1 cup miniature marshmallows	240 ml
½ cup chopped salted peanuts	120 ml

- In bowl, whisk milk and pudding mix for 2 minutes.
- Fold in whipped topping, marshmallows and peanuts.
- Spoon into individual dessert dishes, place plastic wrap over top and chill.

Rice Pudding with Boysenberry Sauce

4 cups whole milk	**1 L**
¾ cup long-grain rice, uncooked	**180 ml**
⅓ cup sugar	**80 ml**
1 large egg	
1 cup boysenberry sauce	**240 ml**

+ Heat milk in medium-heavy saucepan over medium heat. Stir in rice and bring to simmer.
+ Simmer, uncovered, and stir occasionally for 30 minutes or until rice is tender. Remove from heat.
+ In small bowl, whisk sugar and egg. Quickly stir egg mixture into rice mixture. Blend thoroughly and place back on medium heat. Simmer for 1 minute.
+ Remove from heat and spoon into 8 x 8-inch (20 x 20 cm) square baking pan. Cool to room temperature, cover and chill until ready to serve. (Chill at least 1 hour.)
+ To serve, place portion of rice pudding on plate and spoon boysenberry sauce over each portion.

Tip: Prepared boysenberry sauce is available in grocery stores or the recipe is on page 264.

Crunchy Rice Pudding

¼ cup (½ stick) butter, softened	60 ml
1 cup crispy rice cereal	240 ml
1 cup packed brown sugar	240 ml
1 cup apple pie filling	240 ml
1 (22 ounce) carton refrigerated rice pudding	624 g

+ Preheat oven to 350° (176° C).
+ Combine butter, rice cereal and brown sugar, mix well and set aside.
+ Place 3 tablespoons (45 ml) pie filling in each of 6 small, oven-ready custard dishes and divide rice pudding evenly into the 6 dishes.
+ Divide butter mixture evenly into each dish.
+ Place dishes on baking sheet and bake for 15 minutes. Serve warm.

Cherry Trifle

1 (12 ounce) prepared pound cake	340 g
⅓ cup amaretto liqueur	80 ml
2 (20 ounce) cans cherry pie filling, divided	2 (567 g)
4 cups vanilla pudding, divided	1.1 L
1 (8 ounce) carton whipped topping	227 g

+ Cut cake into 1-inch (2.5 cm) slices.
+ Line bottom of 3-quart (3 L) trifle bowl with cake and brush with amaretto.
+ Top with 1 cup (240 ml) pie filling followed by 1 cup (240 ml) pudding. Repeat layers 3 times.
+ Top with whipped topping and chill several hours.

Cinnamon Cream
This dessert must be made the day before serving.

1 (14.4 ounce) box cinnamon graham crackers, divided	410 g
2 (5.1 ounce) packages instant French vanilla pudding mix	2(143 g)
3 cups milk	710 ml
1 (8 ounce) carton whipped topping	227 g
1 (16 ounce) carton prepared caramel icing	.5 kg

+ Line bottom of 9 x 13-inch (23 x 33 cm) casserole dish with one-third of graham crackers.
+ With mixer, combine vanilla pudding and milk and whip until thick and creamy. Fold in whipped topping.
+ Pour half pudding mixture over graham crackers.
+ Top with another layer of graham crackers and add remaining pudding mixture.
+ Top with final layer of graham crackers. (You will have a few crackers left.) Spread frosting over last layer of graham crackers and refrigerate overnight.

Mango Cream

2 soft mangoes	
½ gallon vanilla ice cream, softened	1.8 L
1 (6 ounce) can frozen	
lemonade concentrate, thawed	168 g
1 (8 ounce) carton whipped topping	227 g

- Peel mangoes, cut slices around seeds and cut slices into small chunks.
- In large bowl, mix ice cream, lemonade concentrate and whipped topping and fold in mango chunks.
- Quickly spoon mixture into parfait or sherbet glasses and cover with plastic wrap.
- Place in freezer until ready to serve.

Chocolate-Coconut Mist

2 (14 ounce) packages flaked coconut	2 (396 g)
2 tablespoons (¼ stick) butter,	
softened, optional	30 ml
1⅓ cups semi-sweet chocolate chips, melted	320 ml
3 quarts mint-chocolate chip ice cream	3 L

- Toss coconut, butter and chocolate chips together until they blend well.
- On baking sheet covered with wax paper, shape about ⅓ cupful (80 ml) in 2⅓-inch (6 cm) nests. Chill until firm.
- Just before serving, top each nest with ½ cup (120 ml) ice cream.

Chocolate Cream

12 (1 ounce) squares semi-sweet baking chocolate	12 (28 g)
2 teaspoons vanilla extract	10 ml
1½ cups whipping cream	360 ml
Prepared cream puff shells	

+ In small saucepan, melt chocolate in 4 tablespoons (60 ml) water. Stir constantly until mixture is smooth and all chocolate melts.
+ Stir in vanilla. Remove from heat and set aside to cool.
+ Beat whipping cream until stiff peaks form. Fold chocolate mixture into whipped cream until mixture thoroughly blends and is evenly colored. Chill before serving.
+ Fill cream puff shells using pastry bag or tight plastic bag with corner cut off.

Amaretto Pot de Crème au Chocolat

Pot de Crème (pronounced "poh duh KREHM") is a French phrase meaning "pot of cream". This dessert is a creamy and rich, chocolate-flavored custard prepared and served in tiny pot-shaped cups or custard cups. Although traditionally flavored with vanilla, pot de crème has many variations. Amaretto gives this chocolate version a lovely almond flavor.

4 (1 ounce) squares semi-sweet chocolate	4 (28 g)
1½ cups half-and-half cream	360 ml
6 egg yolks, slightly beaten	
2 tablespoons amaretto liqueur	30 ml

+ Place chocolate and cream in top of double boiler and cook over simmering water until chocolate melts. Stir until mixture is smooth.
+ Spoon some hot chocolate mixture into egg yolks and stir to blend. Add egg yolk mixture to chocolate mixture in double boiler.
+ Add amaretto and continue cooking, stirring constantly, until mixture thickens, about 5 to 6 minutes.
+ Spoon into 8 pot de crème cups or 4 (6 ounce/168 g) custard cups and cool. Chill at least 1 hour and serve.

> *Tip: This is great served with a dollop of whipped cream.*

Mint Chocolate Crème Anglaise

1 cup whipping cream	240 ml
2 cups whole milk	480 ml
5 egg yolks	
6 tablespoons sugar	90 ml
2 (3.5 ounce) premium mint chocolate bars, crumbled	2 (100 g)

- Combine cream and milk in medium saucepan and heat just until bubbles appear around edges.
- While milk mixture heats, whisk egg yolks and sugar in medium bowl. Slowly add hot milk mixture to egg yolks, whisking vigorously, until mixture blends.
- Pour mixture into top of double boiler and cook over very low heat until mixture thickens, about 5 minutes, and coats back of spoon. (It's ready when a finger across spoon leaves trail.) Be careful not to overheat mixture or it will curdle.
- Remove from heat and add chocolate. Whisk until chocolate melts and mixture is smooth.
- Strain mixture into bowl to remove few small solids that may form as it cooks. Cool to room temperature, cover and chill for several hours before serving.
- To serve, spoon into 6 to 8 dessert glasses. Top each with dollop of whipped cream and additional grated chocolate.

Maple Crème Brûlée

4 egg yolks
½ cup maple syrup   **120 ml**
2½ cups half-and-half cream   **600 ml**
2½ teaspoons sugar, divided   **12 ml**

- Preheat oven to 350° (176° C).
- In medium bowl, whisk egg yolks with maple syrup and half-and-half.
- Place 6 crème brûlée dishes or custard cups in large baking dish. Divide egg yolk mixture among custard cups and place on oven rack.
- Pour enough hot water into large baking dish to come halfway up sides of cups.
- Bake for 40 to 45 minutes or until custard sets and knife inserted in middle comes out clean. Remove from water bath and cool on rack. Chill.
- When ready to serve, sprinkle about 1 teaspoon (5 ml) sugar evenly over surface of each and place under broiler.
- Broil until sugar melts slightly and forms crisp coating. Cool again or chill for a few minutes and serve.

White Velvet

1 (8 ounce) carton whipping cream	227 g
1½ teaspoons unflavored gelatin mix	7 ml
⅓ cup sugar	80 ml
1 (8 ounce) carton sour cream	227 g
¾ teaspoon rum flavoring	4 ml

+ Heat cream over moderate heat.
+ Soak gelatin in ¼ cup (60 ml) cold water.
+ When cream is hot, stir in sugar and gelatin until they dissolve and remove from heat. Fold in sour cream and rum flavoring.
+ Pour into individual molds, cover with plastic wrap and chill.
+ Unmold to serve. Serve with fresh fruit.

Coffee Surprise

1 (10 ounce) package large marshmallows	280 g
1 cup strong coffee	240 ml
1 (8 ounce) package chopped dates	227 g
1¼ cups chopped pecans	300 ml
1 (8 ounce) carton whipping cream, whipped	227 g

+ Melt marshmallows in hot coffee. Add dates and pecans and chill.
+ When mixture thickens, fold in whipped cream.
+ Pour into sherbet glasses. Place plastic wrap over top and chill.

This is a super dessert—no slicing, no "dishing up"— just bring it right from the fridge to the table.

Blueberry Fluff

1 (20 ounce) can blueberry pie filling	567 g
1 (20 ounce) can crushed pineapple, drained	567 g
1 (14 ounce) can sweetened condensed milk	396 g
¾ cup chopped pecans	180 ml
1 (8 ounce) carton whipped topping	340 ml

+ Mix pie filling, pineapple, sweetened condensed milk and pecans.
+ Fold in whipped topping.
+ Pour into parfait glasses. Chill.

Grape Fluff

1 cup grape juice	240 ml
2 cups miniature marshmallows	480 ml
2 tablespoons lemon juice	30 ml
1 (8 ounce) carton whipping cream, whipped	227 g

+ In saucepan, heat grape juice to boiling.
+ Add marshmallows and stir constantly until they melt.
+ Add lemon juice and cool.
+ Fold in whipped cream and spoon into individual serving dishes. Chill.

Baked Custard

3 cups milk	710 ml
3 eggs	
¾ cup sugar	180 ml
¼ teaspoon salt	1 ml
1 teaspoon vanilla extract	5 ml

- Heat milk to just before boiling. Beat eggs and add sugar, salt and vanilla.
- Pour scalded milk slowly into egg mixture.
- Pour into 2-quart (2 L) baking dish and sprinkle a little cinnamon on top.
- Bake at 350° (176° C) in hot water bath for 45 minutes.

Boiled Custard

1 (14 ounce) can sweetened condensed milk	396 g
1 quart milk	1 L
4 eggs	
½ teaspoon vanilla extract	2 ml

- Combine both milks and heat in top of double boiler.
- In separate bowl, beat eggs well.
- Slowly pour about ¼ cup (60 ml) milk mixture into eggs and stir constantly.
- Gradually add eggs to remaining milk mixture and cook over low heat for 5 to 10 minutes. Stir constantly until mixture thickens.

This may be served in custard cups or stemmed glasses.

Floating Islands

Also known as "snow eggs", this light classic dessert consists of "islands" of sweetened meringue poached in milk and floated in a custard sauce. It is delightfully simple to make.

3 eggs, separated
11 tablespoons sugar, divided   165 ml
2 tablespoons flour   30 ml
3 cups milk   710 ml
1 teaspoon vanilla extract   5 ml

+ Whisk egg yolks, 5 tablespoons (75 ml) sugar and flour in top of double boiler. Stir in milk.
+ Place double boiler over simmering water and cook until mixture coats back of spoon. Stir in vanilla.
+ Remove from heat and pour mixture into 2-quart (2 L) baking dish.
+ To make meringue, beat egg whites and remaining 6 tablespoons (90 ml) sugar until stiff peaks form.
+ Drop by tablespoons onto cooked custard. Place under broiler and brown slightly. Chill before serving.

Cinnamon-Orange Custard

1 large orange	
⅔ cup sugar	**160 ml**
7 egg yolks	
2 cups whipping cream	**480 ml**
¼ teaspoon cinnamon	**1 ml**

- Preheat oven to 325° (162° C).
- Place 5 (6 ounce) ramekins in 9 x 13-inch (23 x 33 cm) baking dish.
- Grate orange peel to yield 1 tablespoon zest. Squeeze orange to yield ¼ cup (60 ml) juice and set aside.
- In medium bowl, lightly whisk sugar, egg yolks and orange zest. Lightly whisk in cream, cinnamon and orange juice. (Lightly whisk so bubbles will not remain on surface of custard when it cooks.)
- Divide mixture equally among prepared ramekins. Pour hot water into baking dish to reach halfway up sides of ramekins.
- Bake for about 55 minutes or until custard sets around edges but jiggles slightly in center when gently shaken.
- Remove from water bath and cool on rack. Chill for several hours before serving. (These may be made 1 or 2 days in advance.)

> *Optional: If desired, beat ½ cup (120 ml) whipping cream with 1 tablespoon (15 ml) powdered sugar. Spoon dollop of whipped cream on top of each custard just before serving.*

Lemon Curd

4 lemons
1 tablespoon lemon zest   **15 ml**
3 tablespoons butter   **45 ml**
½ cup sugar   **120 ml**
1 large egg, plus 1 large egg yolk

- Sqeeze ⅓ cup (80 ml) juice from lemons and grate peel for zest.
- Place lemon juice, lemon zest, butter and sugar in top of double boiler over gently simmering water.
- Stir until butter melts and sugar dissolves. (Water must be hot enough to melt butter and dissolve sugar, but not too hot or eggs will cook when you add them in the next step.)
- Beat whole egg and egg yolk in separate bowl and slowly add them to lemon mixture in pan. Stir quickly and thoroughly as eggs are added.
- Pour mixture into small, heavy saucepan and place over low heat. Cook and stir frequently until mixture thickens, about 5 to 6 minutes. (Mixture should coat back of spoon and a trail left when your finger runs across it.)
- Remove from heat and cool. Cover and chill.
  Yield: 1 cup (240 ml).

Sunny Citrus-Mango Mousse

This lovely orange-colored mousse has a delicate citrus flavor. Because it is refreshing and cool, but not overly sweet, it makes a terrific summertime dessert.

2 oranges
1 cup sugar   **240 ml**
1 (.25 ounce) packet unflavored gelatin mix   **7 g**
3 cups whipping cream   **710 ml**
1 very ripe mango, peeled, puréed

+ Squeeze juice from 2 oranges to equal ½ (120 ml) cup. Add a little water if necessary. Grate orange peel to yield 2 teaspoons (10 ml) zest.
+ Place juice and orange zest in small saucepan and cook over low heat. Stir in ⅓ cup (80 ml) water and sugar.
+ Cook and stir until sugar dissolves and remove from heat.
+ Stir gelatin into ¼ cup (60 ml) cold water until it dissolves. Add to orange mixture and stir to blend. Set aside to cool.
+ Beat cream until soft peaks form. Fold in cooled orange-gelatin mixture until they blend well and gently fold in puréed mango.
+ Place mousse mixture in lightly greased mold and chill several hours until firm. Turn mold onto serving plate just before serving.

> *Tip: Any decorative mold will make this a beautiful dish. (I use a small bundt pan with decorative sides.) To oil mold, place ½ teaspoon (2 ml) oil into mold and spread with paper towel to coat all indentations.*

Fresh Strawberry Mousse

When red, ripe strawberries are in season, they
make this light, summery dessert a showpiece.

1 (.25 ounce) packet unflavored gelatin mix	7 g
2 cups hulled, sliced strawberries	
plus a few whole ones	480 ml
¼ cup plus 3 tablespoons sugar, divided	60 ml; 45 ml
1 cup whipping cream	240 ml

+ Pour ¼ cup (60 ml) cold water in small saucepan and sprinkle gelatin over water. Stir over low heat until gelatin dissolves, about 1 minute. Remove from heat.
+ Set aside whole strawberries for garnish.
+ Put sliced strawberries, ¼ cup (60 ml) sugar and gelatin mixture in blender or food processor and purée.
+ Pour mixture into bowl and chill for 1 hour to thicken.
+ Place remaining 3 tablespoons (45 ml) sugar and whipping cream in bowl and beat on high speed until soft peaks form.
+ Fold chilled strawberry mixture into whipped cream a little at a time until mousse blends well.
+ Garnish with fresh strawberries. Chill until ready to serve.

Kahlua Mousse

Light but rich and absolutely delicious!

1 (12 ounce) carton whipped topping	340 g
2 teaspoons dry instant coffee granules	10 ml
5 teaspoons cocoa	25 ml
5 tablespoons sugar	75 ml
½ cup kahlua liqueur	120 ml

+ In large bowl, combine whipped topping, coffee, cocoa and sugar and blend well.
+ Fold in kahlua and spoon into sherbet dessert glasses.
+ Place plastic wrap over dessert glasses until ready to serve.

Cappuccino Mousse

2 teaspoons instant coffee granules	10 ml
1 (14 ounce) can sweetened condensed milk	396 g
⅓ cup cocoa	80 ml
3 tablespoons butter	15 ml
2 cups cold whipping cream	480 ml

+ Dissolve instant coffee in 2 teaspoons (10 ml) water.
+ Combine sweetened condensed milk, cocoa, butter and coffee in saucepan. Cook over low heat, stirring constantly, until butter melts and mixture is smooth.
+ Remove from heat and cool.
+ In large bowl, beat whipping cream until stiff. Gradually fold coffee mixture into cream.
+ Spoon into dessert dishes and chill until set.

Creamy Chocolate Mousse

*What a dreamy delight! This thick, velvety
smooth mousse is a favorite every time.*

1 (12 ounce) package semi-sweet chocolate chips	340 g
3 cups whipping cream, divided	710 ml
2 tablespoons orange liqueur	45 ml
⅓ cup powdered sugar	80 ml

- Combine chocolate chips and 1 cup (240 ml) whipping cream in heavy, medium saucepan.
- Cook over low to medium heat, stirring constantly, until chocolate melts and mixture is smooth.
- Stir in orange liqueur. Set aside and cool to room temperature.
- In large bowl, beat remaining 2 cups (480 ml) whipping cream and powdered sugar until stiff peaks form.
- Gently fold chocolate mixture into whipped cream until it blends well and is evenly colored.
- Spoon into 8 dessert cups. Cover and chill for several hours or until ready to serve.

*Optional: For a really nice finish, garnish each dessert
with a pretty cookie such as a pirouette to give it a little
extra flair. Or, top with a dollop of whipped cream and
place a chocolate-dipped, candied orange peel on top.*

Quick-and-Easy
Chocolate Mousse

1 (.25 ounce) packet unflavored gelatin mix	.7 g
½ cup light corn syrup	120 ml
1 (6 ounce) package semi-sweet chocolate chips	168 g
1 teaspoon vanilla extract	5 ml
1 pint whipping cream, whipped	.5 kg

+ In saucepan, sprinkle gelatin over ¼ cup (60 ml) water and let stand 2 minutes.
+ Add corn syrup and cook, stirring constantly, for 5 minutes over low heat. Remove from heat and stir in chocolate chips and vanilla until smooth.
+ Gently fold chocolate mixture into whipped cream and spoon into individual serving bowls. Refrigerate.

White Chocolate-Mocha Mousse Parfaits

1 cup milk chocolate chips	240 ml
3 cups whipping cream, divided	710 ml
1 tablespoon instant coffee granules	15 ml
1 cup white chocolate chips	240 ml
⅓ cup powdered sugar	80 ml

+ In small saucepan, combine milk chocolate chips, ½ cup (120 ml) whipping cream and instant coffee. Cook over low to medium heat, stirring constantly, until chocolate melts and mixture is smooth. Set aside.
+ Repeat with white chocolate chips and ½ cup (120 ml) whipping cream. Set aside.
+ Let both mixtures cool to room temperature.
+ In large bowl, beat remaining 2 cups (480 ml) whipping cream and powdered sugar until stiff peaks form.
+ Divide whipped cream mixture in half and gently fold half into chocolate mixture until they blend well and mixture is evenly colored. Fold other half into white chocolate mixture until they blend well.
+ Divide half white chocolate mixture among 6 or 8 parfait glasses. Top with half chocolate mixture divided evenly among glasses.
+ Repeat layers with white chocolate and chocolate mousse. Each cup will have 4 alternating layers of mousse.

Optional: For a special finish, top each one off with dollop of whipped cream and a few chocolate-coated coffee beans as garnish.

Butter Pecan-Pumpkin Parfait

Try this for a change in the fall. It is a
fun, chilled dessert at any time.

1 (20 ounce) can pumpkin pie filling, divided	567 g
1 quart vanilla or butter pecan ice cream	1 kg
½ cup flaked coconut, toasted	120 ml
½ cup finely chopped pecans	120 ml
Dash nutmeg and cinnamon	

- Chill pumpkin pie filling overnight.
- Just before serving, carefully spoon about 2 tablespoons (30 ml) pie filling into each of 6 parfait glasses.
- Add small scoop ice cream and sprinkle toasted coconut and chopped pecans on top. Repeat layers.
- Top with dashes of nutmeg and cinnamon over last layer.

Honey-Rice Pudding Parfaits

12 cinnamon graham crackers, crushed, divided
1 (22 ounce) carton refrigerated rice pudding   **624 g**
½ cup honey   **120 ml**
Fresh strawberries

- Spoon 2 heaping tablespoons (30 ml) cracker crumbs into each of 5 sherbet or parfait glasses.
- In bowl, mix rice pudding and honey and divide evenly into glasses.
- Sprinkle remaining crushed graham crackers over top of rice pudding mixture and place 4 or 5 strawberries on top.
- Refrigerate. (If you like, use raspberries instead of strawberries.)

Banana Crunch Parfaits

Here's a 5-minute recipe for some very attractive and tasty parfaits. The parfaits combine crunchy toffee and buttery shortbread with creamy pudding and bananas. Top all that off with whipped cream and toffee and it's pretty impressive for 5-minutes' work!

½ cup crushed shortbread cookies	120 ml
6 (3.5 ounce) containers vanilla pudding, divided	6 (100 g)
1½ bananas	
½ cup crushed chocolate-covered toffee candy bars, divided	120 ml
1 cup frozen whipped topping, thawed or whipped cream	240 ml

+ Divide shortbread cookie crumbs evenly in bottom of 6 parfait glasses.
+ Using 3 pudding containers, spoon half a container of vanilla pudding over crumbs in each glass.
+ Cut bananas in thick slices and divide them evenly on top of vanilla pudding.
+ Sprinkle toffee pieces over bananas, but reserve a few teaspoonfuls for garnish.
+ Use remaining 3 pudding containers to place half a container of pudding over toffee.
+ Divide whipped topping among glasses and place dollop in center of each glass.
+ Sprinkle reserved toffee over whipped topping for garnish. Keep chilled until ready to serve.

Lemon-Raspberry Parfaits

What a quick, easy 5-minute recipe!

1 cup whipping cream, chilled	240 ml
⅓ cup lemon-flavored yogurt	80 ml
⅓ cup sugar	80 ml
2 bananas	
1 (12 ounce or smaller) bag frozen, sweetened raspberries or 1 pint fresh raspberries	340 g; .5 kg

- In mixing bowl, beat whipping cream with yogurt and sugar until soft peaks form.
- Divide half of mixture into 4 parfait glasses.
- Slice bananas and arrange layer on top of whipped cream mixture in each glass.
- Top with remaining cream mixture divided equally among glasses.
- Sprinkle raspberries over top of parfait. Chill until ready to serve.

Blueberry-Pudding Parfaits

2 cups (1 pint) fresh blueberries, divided	**480 ml**
½ cup sugar	**120 ml**
1 tablespoon cornstarch	**15 ml**
1 (22 ounce) container prepared vanilla pudding	**624 g**

- Reserve 6 blueberries for garnish and place remaining blueberries in medium saucepan with ½ cup (120 ml) water.
- Bring to simmer and cook, covered, over medium heat for 12 to 15 minutes or until blueberries are soft.
- Remove from heat and place half blueberries in bowl. Mash blueberries in bowl with potato masher or back of spoon to release juice. Strain, squeeze out as much juice as possible and discard pulp.
- Return blueberry juice to saucepan with remaining half blueberries and add sugar.
- Mix cornstarch with 1 tablespoon (15 ml) cool water to make paste and stir paste into blueberry mixture.
- Bring blueberry mixture to simmer again and cook over low heat until mixture thickens, about 4 to 6 minutes. Stir carefully to avoid crushing whole blueberries.
- Remove from heat and cool to room temperature.
- Divide half pudding evenly among 6 small or 4 large dessert cups. Place 1 tablespoon (15 ml) blueberry sauce over pudding in each cup.
- Repeat layers with remaining pudding and sauce on top with reserved fresh blueberries.

Optional: Top with whipped cream before garnishing with reserved fresh blueberries.

Fruits
&
Smoothies

Brandied Fruit

2 (20 ounce) cans crushed pineapple	2 (567 g)
1 (16 ounce) can sliced peaches	.5 kg
2 (11 ounce) cans mandarin oranges	2 (312 g)
1 (10 ounce) jar maraschino cherries	280 g
Sugar	
1 cup brandy	240 ml

+ Let all fruit drain for 12 hours.
+ For every cup of drained fruit, add ½ cup (120 ml) sugar. Let stand 12 hours.
+ Add brandy, spoon into large jar and store in refrigerator.
+ This mixture needs to stand in refrigerator for 3 weeks.
+ Serve over ice cream.

Brandied Apples

1 (10 ounce) pound cake loaf	280 g
1 (20 ounce) can apple pie filling	567 g
½ teaspoon allspice	2 ml
2 tablespoons brandy	30 ml
Vanilla ice cream	

+ Slice pound cake and place on dessert plates.
+ In saucepan, combine pie filling, allspice and brandy. Heat and stir just until heated thoroughly.
+ Place several spoonfuls over cake and top with scoop of vanilla ice cream.

Amaretto Peaches

4½ cups peeled, sliced fresh peaches	**1.1 L**
½ cup amaretto liqueur	**120 ml**
½ cup sour cream	**120 ml**
½ cup packed brown sugar	**120 ml**

+ Lay peaches in 2-quart (2 L) baking dish.
+ Pour amaretto over peaches and spread with sour cream.
+ Sprinkle brown sugar evenly over all.
+ Broil mixture until it heats thoroughly and sugar melts.

Peachy Sundaes

1 pint vanilla ice cream	**.5 kg**
¾ cup peach preserves, warmed	**180 ml**
¼ cup chopped almonds, toasted	**60 ml**
¼ cup flaked coconut	**60 ml**

+ Divide ice cream into 4 sherbet dishes.
+ Top with preserves.
+ Sprinkle with almonds and coconut.

Brandied Cherries

You cannot beat this simple dessert when you want to enjoy ripe cherries in the peak of the season. If you like, add an apricot or two with the cherries for a little variety.

½ cup sugar	120 ml
¼ cup brandy	60 ml
2 pounds cherries, pitted	1 kg
2 tablespoons lemon juice	30 ml

+ Combine sugar and brandy in medium saucepan.
+ Add cherries and lemon juice. Bring to simmer and stir occasionally until sugar dissolves.
+ Cook cherries over medium heat until tender, about 5 minutes. Serve warm over ice cream or angel food cake.

Cherry Delight

This is a great fruity dessert and it only takes 5 minutes to make.

1 (20 ounce) can pineapple chunks with juice	567 g
2 bananas	
1 (20 ounce) can cherry pie filling	567 g
1 (11 ounce) can mandarin oranges, drained	312 g
¼ cup chopped pecans	60 ml

+ Drain pineapple juice into bowl. Slice bananas and dip slices in pineapple juice.
+ Gently combine all ingredients. Chill for 1 hour.

This dessert is best served chilled, so if you want to make it just before serving, you should chill all the ingredients beforehand.

Bing Cherry Shortcakes

½ pound bing cherries, pitted — 227 g
½ cup plus 2 tablespoons sugar, divided — 120 ml; 30 ml
⅔ cup whipping cream — 160 ml
2 tablespoons cherry liqueur — 30 ml
4 sponge cakes

+ Bring cherries, ½ cup (120 ml) water and ½ cup (120 ml) sugar to simmer in medium saucepan and cook for 4 to 5 minutes. Remove from heat and cool.
+ In chilled bowl, whip cream, remaining 2 tablespoons (30 ml) sugar and cherry liqueur until stiff peaks form.
+ Spoon cherries and syrup over each shortcake and top with whipped cream mixture before serving.

Strawberry Trifle

1 (5 ounce) package instant
   French vanilla pudding mix — 140 g
1 (10 ounce) loaf pound cake, sliced — 280 g
2 cups fresh strawberries, sliced — 480 ml
½ cup sherry, divided — 120 ml
Whipped topping

+ Prepare pudding according to package directions.
+ Place layer of pound cake slices in 8-inch (20 cm) crystal bowl and sprinkle with ¼ cup (60 ml) sherry.
+ Add layer of strawberries and layer half pudding.
+ Repeat layers and chill overnight or several hours.
+ Before serving, top with whipped topping.

Creamy Strawberry Punch

1 (10 ounce) package
   frozen strawberries, thawed   280 g
½ gallon strawberry ice cream, softened   1.8 L
2 (2 liter) bottles ginger ale, chilled   2 (2 L)
Fresh strawberries, optional

- Process frozen strawberries in blender.
- Combine strawberries, chunks of ice cream and ginger ale in punch bowl.
- Stir and serve immediately.
- Garnish with fresh strawberries.

Pineapple-Strawberry Cooler

2 cups milk   480 ml
1 (20 ounce) can crushed pineapple, chilled   567 g
½ pint vanilla ice cream   227 g
1 pint strawberry ice cream   .5 kg

- In mixing bowl, combine milk, pineapple and vanilla ice cream.
- Mix just until they blend.
- Pour into tall glasses and top with scoop of strawberry ice cream.

Fruits

Strawberries Topped with Sweetened Mascarpone

This simple, 5-minute dessert is refreshing and delicious, especially when made with flavorful, ripe strawberries. It is an excellent end to a hearty meal.

1 cup whipping cream, chilled	240 ml
½ cup mascarpone cheese, softened	120 ml
¼ cup sugar	60 ml
2 tablespoons sweet marsala wine	30 ml
1 pound fresh strawberries, hulled, thickly quartered	.5 kg

+ In mixing bowl, combine whipping cream, mascarpone cheese, sugar and wine. Beat on high speed until soft peaks form.
+ Divide strawberries between 6 to 8 custard or dessert cups. Top with cream mixture divided equally among the dessert cups.

Tip: If you can't find mascarpone, you can substitute Neufchatel or cream cheese.

Pudding Dip for Strawberries

1 (3.4 ounce) package instant French vanilla pudding mix	98 g
1 cup milk	240 ml
¼ cup sugar	60 ml
1 (8 ounce) carton sour cream	227 g
¾ teaspoon almond extract	4 ml

- Beat pudding mix, milk and sugar until ingredients blend well.
- Stir in sour cream and almond extract.
- Refrigerate several hours and serve over fresh strawberries.

Strawberry Smoothie

2 medium bananas, peeled, sliced	
1 pint fresh strawberries, washed, quartered	.5 kg
1 (8 ounce) container strawberry yogurt	227 g
¼ cup orange juice	60 ml

- Place all ingredients in blender and process until smooth.
- Serve as is or over crushed ice.

Strawberries in the Clouds

1 (8 ounce) package cream cheese, softened	227 g
1 tablespoon amaretto liqueur	15 ml
1 (16 ounce) box powdered sugar	.5 kg
1 (8 ounce) carton whipped topping	227 g

+ Beat cream cheese and amaretto until creamy and add powdered sugar.
+ Gently fold in whipped topping.

> *You may serve a dollop of this creamy mixture over a bowl of sweetened strawberries or use it as a dip for whole strawberries.*

Divine Strawberries

1 quart fresh strawberries	1 L
1 (20 ounce) can pineapple chunks, well drained	567 g
2 bananas, sliced	
1 (18 ounce) carton strawberry glaze	510 g

+ Cut strawberries in half (or in quarters if strawberries are very large).
+ Add pineapple chunks and banana slices.
+ Fold in strawberry glaze and chill.

> *This is wonderful over pound cake or just served in sherbet glasses.*

Chocolate-Covered Strawberries

2 to 3 pints fresh strawberries with stems	**1 - 1.5 kg**
1 (12 ounce) package semi-sweet chocolate chips	**227 g**
2 tablespoons shortening	**30 ml**

- Make sure strawberries are clean and dry.
- In small, heavy saucepan over low heat, melt chocolate chips and shortening and stir constantly until mixture blends and is smooth. Cool slightly.
- Hold strawberries by top and dip two-thirds of each strawberry into chocolate mixture. Over saucepan, drip excess chocolate off strawberry.
- Place strawberries on tray covered with wax paper. After all strawberries are dipped, chill until chocolate sets and is firm, about 1 hour.
- Remove from tray, cover and chill until ready to serve.

Chocolate-Dipped Stuffed Dates

Although it sometimes seems that adding anything at all to these luscious dates is "gilding the lily" (because they are fabulous just by themselves), this is a truly exquisite treat with the addition of nuts and chocolate. This date recipe makes a great finger food because it is easy and neat to eat.

24 Medjool dates
24 walnut halves
3 ounces semi-sweet chocolate, melted   **84 g**

+ With paring knife, slice each date down one side and remove pit. Insert walnut half.
+ Dip the bottom half of each stuffed date in melted chocolate and place on wax paper or foil to set.

> *Tip: If you cut from one end of the date toward the stem end, the pit may be easily pushed out by the knife as you slice.*

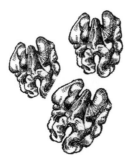

Chocolate Fruit Dip

1 (8 ounce) package cream cheese, softened	227 g
¼ cup chocolate syrup	60 ml
1 (7 ounce) jar marshmallow cream	98 g
Fruit	

- In mixing bowl, beat cream cheese and chocolate syrup until smooth.
- Fold in marshmallow cream.
- Cover and chill until ready to serve.

  Serve with apple wedges, banana chunks or strawberries.

Easy Chocolate Dessert Fondue

1 (12 ounce) package semi-sweet chocolate chips	340 g
¾ cup half-and-half cream	180 ml
½ cup sugar	120 ml
Strawberries, mandarin orange sections, cherries, bananas	

- In heavy saucepan, melt chocolate chips, half-and-half and sugar over medium heat. Stir constantly until chocolate melts and mixture blends well.
- Pour into fondue pot and serve with fruit for dipping. Yield: about 2 cups (480 ml).

Peachy Fruit Dip

1 (15 ounce) can sliced peaches, drained	425 g
½ cup marshmallow cream	120 ml
1 (3 ounce) package cream cheese, softened, cubed	84 g
⅛ teaspoon ground nutmeg	.5 ml

+ In blender or food processor, combine all ingredients.
+ Serve with assorted fresh fruit.

Winter-Peach Dessert

1 (15 ounce) can sliced peaches with juice	425 g
¼ cup grenadine	60 ml
¼ cup sugar	60 ml
1 cup crumbled coconut macaroons	240 ml

+ Drain peaches and reserve ¼ cup (60 ml) juice.
+ In saucepan, combine peaches, reserved juice, grenadine and sugar.
+ Bring to boil, reduce heat, simmer 6 minutes and turn peach slices to coat with syrup.
+ Gently stir in crumbled macaroons over low heat until liquid absorbs by macaroons.
+ Serve warm in sherbet dishes.

Sugared Peaches with Sweet Marsala Wine Sauce

What a great way to enjoy fresh peaches! Sweet tender peaches are covered in a delicate wine sauce flavored with tiny currants.

¼ cup dried currants	60 ml
½ cup orange juice	120 ml
½ cup sweet marsala wine	120 ml
6 tablespoons sugar, divided	90 ml
2 large peaches, peeled, pitted, sliced into ¼-inch (.6 cm) slices	

+ Place currants, orange juice, wine and 4 tablespoons (60 ml) sugar in medium saucepan.
+ Bring to boil and cook, stirring frequently, over medium heat until syrupy, about 10 minutes.
+ While sauce cooks, place peaches in shallow baking dish or on tray. Sprinkle with remaining 2 tablespoons (30 ml) sugar and place under broiler.
+ Broil for 2 to 3 minutes until sugar melts and slightly browns. (Watch carefully so they don't burn.) Remove from oven.
+ Place peach slices on plate, drizzle sauce over slices and serve. Yield: 4 servings.

> *Optional: To add even more flavor to this dish, put a cinnamon stick in the sauce with other ingredients and discard it when you remove sauce from heat.*

Orange-Pear Salad

1 (15 ounce) can sliced pears with juice	425 g
1 (6 ounce) package orange gelatin mix	168 g
1 (8 ounce) package cream cheese, softened	227 g
1 (8 ounce) carton whipped topping	227 g

- Boil juice from pears with ½ cup (120 ml) water, add gelatin and stir until it dissolves.
- Chill until partially set.
- Blend pears and cream cheese in blender.
- Fold pear mixture and whipped topping into gelatin mixture and blend well.
- Pour into 7 x 11-inch (18 x 28 ml) shallow dish.

Spiced Pears

1 (15 ounce) can pear halves	425 g
⅓ cup packed brown sugar	80 ml
¾ teaspoon ground nutmeg	180 ml
¾ teaspoon ground cinnamon	180 ml

- Drain pears, reserve syrup and set pears aside.
- Place syrup, brown sugar, nutmeg and cinnamon in saucepan and bring to a boil.
- Reduce heat and simmer uncovered for 5 to 8 minutes. Stir frequently.
- Add pears and simmer for 5 minutes longer or until mixture heats through.

Pears Poached in Wine

4 firm, ripe pears
2 tablespoons lemon juice   **30 ml**
1 cup sweet marsala wine   **240 ml**
⅓ cup sugar   **80 ml**

- Peel pears and carefully remove core from bottom end leaving stem end intact. Set aside.
- Combine lemon juice, wine, 2 cups (480 ml) hot water and sugar in 2-quart (2 L) saucepan.
- Bring liquid to boil and add pears standing with stem up. Add more hot water, if necessary, to make liquid just cover pears.
- Return to boil and simmer, covered, for about 15 minutes or until pears are tender. Remove pears and place them in dish with high sides.
- Return liquid to rapid boil and reduce to about 1 cup (240 ml). (This may take about 30 minutes, depending upon how much liquid is used.)
- Pour liquid over pears and cool. Serve at room temperature or chilled.

Apple-Spiced Pears

4 medium pears
½ cup firmly packed brown sugar   **120 ml**
1 teaspoon apple pie spice   **5 ml**

+ Preheat oven to 350° (176° C).
+ Peel and core pears. Slice in half vertically and place in 9 x 13-inch (23 x 33 cm) baking dish.
+ Score each pear by making 6 or 7 vertical and horizontal slices and set aside.
+ In small saucepan, combine brown sugar, ¼ cup (60 ml) water and apple pie spice. Cook over medium heat until sugar dissolves.
+ Pour sugar mixture over pears. Cover with foil and bake for 45 minutes. Remove from oven, cool and serve.

Honeyed Pears

2 (15 ounce) cans pear halves, drained	2 (425 g)
¼ cup (½ stick) butter, melted	60 ml
½ cup honey	120 ml
1 cup crushed macaroons or butter cookies	240 ml

+ Preheat oven to 350° (176° C).
+ Place pear halves in single layer in 11 x 7-inch (28 x 18 cm) or 9 x 9-inch (23 x 23 cm) baking dish.
+ In small bowl, combine butter with honey and pour over pears.
+ Bake, uncovered, for 20 minutes.
+ Sprinkle crushed cookies over pears and bake for another 10 minutes. Serve warm.

Wine-Soaked Nectarines

¼ cup sugar	60 ml
1¾ cups white zinfandel or riesling wine	420 ml
6 large nectarines, halved, pitted	
1 pint raspberries, washed, dried	.5 kg

+ In large bowl, stir sugar into wine until it dissolves. Slice nectarines into ¼-inch (.6 cm) pieces and gently place nectarines and raspberries in wine mixture.
+ Cover and let stand at room temperature for at least 2 hours before serving. Chill for up to 6 hours and bring to room temperature before serving.

Fruit Dip for Nectarines

1 (8 ounce) package cream cheese, softened	227 g
2 (7 ounce) cartons marshmallow cream	2 (198 g)
¼ teaspoon cinnamon	1 ml
⅛ teaspoon ground ginger	.5 ml

+ Use mixer to combine and beat all ingredients.
+ Mix well and chill.
+ Serve with unpeeled slices of nectarines or any other fruit.

Tropical Smoothie

1½ heaping cups peeled, seeded ripe papaya	360 ml
1 very ripe large banana	
1½ heaping cups ripe cantaloupe	360 ml
1 (6 ounce) carton coconut cream pie yogurt	168 g
¼ cup milk	60 ml

+ Cut papaya into chunks.
+ Place all ingredients in blender and puree until smooth.
+ Pour into glasses and serve immediately.

Banana-Mango Smoothie

1 cup peeled, cubed ripe mango	240 ml
1 ripe banana, sliced	
⅔ cup milk	160 ml
1 teaspoon honey	5 ml
¼ teaspoon vanilla extract	1 ml

+ Arrange mango cubes in single layer on baking sheet and freeze about 1 hour or until firm.
+ Combine frozen mango, banana, milk, honey and vanilla and pour into blender.
+ Process until smooth.

Watermelon Smoothie

2 cups cubed, seeded watermelon	480 ml
2 tablespoons honey	30 ml
Dash cinnamon	
1 (8 ounce) carton lemon yogurt	227 g

- In blender, purée watermelon, honey and cinnamon quickly so as not to overblend.
- Pulse in lemon yogurt and serve immediately.

Fruit Smoothie

1 cup orange juice	240 ml
1 ripe banana, peeled, thickly sliced	
1 ripe peach, cubed	
1 cup strawberries	240 ml

- Put orange juice into blender.
- Add banana, peach, strawberries and 1 cup (240 ml) ice cubes.
- Blend on high speed until liquefied.

Not-So-Sweet Dessert Salad

*To have this dessert ready in 5 minutes, chill all
the ingredients first. When it is time to serve,
just combine and you're ready to go!*

1 (1 pint) carton cottage cheese, drained	.5 kg
1 (8 ounce) carton frozen	
whipped topping, thawed	227 g
½ cup chopped pecans	120 ml
1 (20 ounce) can chunk pineapple, drained	567 g
1 (11 ounce) can mandarin oranges, drained	312 g

+ Combine cottage cheese and whipped topping in large
  bowl. Mix until they blend well.
+ Stir in pecans and fold in pineapple and oranges. Serve
  chilled.

Fruit Medley

2 cups red grapes, halved	480 ml
2 cups green grapes, halved	480 ml
2 cups cubed honeydew melon, chilled	480 ml
1 (20 ounce) can pineapple tidbits,	
drained, chilled	567 g
1 banana, sliced	
¾ cup peach preserves, chilled	180 ml

+ In large salad bowl, combine grapes, melon, pineapple and
  banana. Whisk in peach preserves and toss to coat.
+ Chill before serving.

Berry Salad Dream

1 (15 ounce) can crushed pineapple with juice	425 g
1 (6 ounce) package blackberry gelatin mix	168 g
1 (15 ounce) can blueberries, drained	425 g
Whipped topping, optional	

+ Add enough water to pineapple juice to make 2 cups (480 ml), put in saucepan and bring to a boil.
+ Pour hot liquid over gelatin and mix until it dissolves.
+ Chill until this mixture begins to thicken.
+ Stir in pineapple and blueberries, pour into 7 x 11-inch (18 x 28 cm) dish and chill.

Topping:

1 (8 ounce) package cream cheese, softened	227 g
1 (8 ounce) carton sour cream	227 g
½ cup sugar	120 ml
½ cup chopped pecans	120 ml

+ Use mixer to beat cream cheese, sour cream and sugar until smooth and fluffy.
+ Pour over congealed salad and chill.
+ Sprinkle with pecans before serving.

Stained-Glass Salad

1 (11 ounce) can mandarin oranges, drained	312 g
1 (10 ounce) package frozen strawberries, thawed	280 g
1 (8 ounce) can pineapple tidbits, drained	227 g
1 (15 ounce) can pears, drained, sliced	425 g
1 (20 ounce) can peach pie filling	567 g

- Pour all ingredients into serving bowl and chill.
- Serve over pound cake or by itself in dessert dishes.

Salad Supreme

1 (6 ounce) package orange gelatin mix	168 g
1 (8 ounce) package cream cheese, softened	227 g
2 (15 ounce) cans mangoes with juice	2 (425 g)
2 (10 ounce) cans mandarin oranges, drained	2 (280 g)

- Place gelatin in mixing bowl, add ¾ cup (180 ml) boiling water and mix well.
- Cool gelatin partially and, beginning at very slow speed, beat in cream cheese until it mixes.
- Fold in mangoes and mandarin oranges.
- Pour into 8 1-cup/8 (240 ml) molds and chill for several hours.

Glazed Fruit Salad

2 (11 ounce) cans mandarin oranges, drained	2 (312 g)
1 (15 ounce) can pineapple chunks, drained	425 g
3 bananas, sliced	
1 (18 ounce) carton creamy glaze for bananas	510 g

+ In large bowl, combine all ingredients.
+ Toss to coat fruit and serve immediately.

Tip: Grapes, apples or marshmallows could also be added to this salad.

Sweet Surrender

It's nice to serve this dessert in sherbet dishes with a sugar cookie.

1 (14 ounce) can sweetened condensed milk	396 g
¼ cup lemon juice	60 ml
1 (20 ounce) can coconut pie filling, chilled	567 g
1 (15 ounce) can pineapple tidbits, drained, chilled	425 g
1 (15 ounce) can fruit cocktail, drained, chilled	426 g
1 (8 ounce) carton whipped topping	227 g

+ In large bowl, combine sweetened condensed milk and lemon juice.
+ Stir in pie filling, pineapple and fruit cocktail.
+ Fold in whipped topping and refrigerate.

Spirit Sweet Fruit

2 cups peeled, cubed ripe mango	480 ml
2 cups peeled, cubed kiwi fruit	480 ml
2 cups peeled, cubed fresh pineapple	480 ml
¼ cup flaked coconut	60 ml

Dressing:

½ cup sugar	120 ml
¼ teaspoon ground cinnamon	1 ml
¼ cup white rum	60 ml
3 tablespoons lime juice	45 ml

+ In large bowl, combine mango, kiwi and pineapple. Refrigerate until fruit chills well.
+ In saucepan, combine sugar, cinnamon and ½ cup (120 ml) water, bring to boil and cook 1 minute.
+ Stir in rum and lime juice and cool completely. Pour dressing over fruit and gently toss.
+ Serve in pretty sherbet glasses and sprinkle coconut over top.

Fresh Fruit with Hawaiian Glaze

You choose the fresh fruit you enjoy most: bananas, strawberries, pineapple, melon, kiwi, nectarines, peaches, apples, grapes and more. Add the Hawaiian Glaze below for a beautiful, refreshing dessert.

Hawaiian Glaze:
1 lemon
2 cups pineapple or orange-pineapple juice 480 ml
3 tablespoons sugar 45 ml
1 tablespoon cornstarch 15 ml
Whipped cream

+ Squeeze 1 tablespoon (15 ml) juice from lemon and grate peel to yield ½ teaspoon (2 ml) zest. Set aside.
+ In medium saucepan, combine pineapple juice, sugar, cornstarch, lemon juice and lemon peel.
+ Cook over medium high heat and bring to boil. Reduce heat and continue to cook until sauce begins to thicken.
+ Arrange fruit slices in individual cups and pour glaze, warm or chilled, over fruit. Top with whipped cream.

Fresh Fruit with Orange Sauce

This may be served as a dessert or with breakfast.

2 cups fresh pineapple chunks or canned pineapple, drained	480 ml
2 cups cubed cantaloupe	480 ml
2 cups strawberries	480 ml
2 cups green grapes	480 ml
2 cups cubed honeydew melon	480 ml
2 cups fresh blueberries or canned blueberries, drained	480 ml

Orange Sauce:	
1½ cups orange juice	360 ml
½ cup sugar	120 ml
1 teaspoon vanilla extract	5 ml

- Combine all fruit in bowl with lid.
- Place all sauce ingredients in jar with lid and shake until sugar dissolves.
- Pour sauce over fruit, cover and refrigerate overnight.

Fun Fruit Fajitas

1 (20 ounce) can cherry pie filling	567 g
8 large flour tortillas	
1½ cups sugar	360 ml
¾ cup (1½ sticks) butter	180 ml
1 teaspoon almond flavoring	5 ml

+ Divide fruit equally on tortillas, roll up and place in 9 x 13-inch (23 x 33 cm) baking dish.
+ Mix sugar and butter in saucepan with 2 cups (480 ml) water and bring to boil.
+ Add almond flavoring and pour over flour tortillas.
+ Place in refrigerator and soak 1 to 24 hours.
+ Bake at 350° (176° C) for 20 minutes or until brown and bubbly. Serve hot or room temperature.

Use any flavor of pie filling you like.

Red, White and Gooey Banana Splits

Sometimes we forget the simplest things, so we added this to our collection. The fun part is in the variations we suggest and you invent.

1 firm banana
1 scoop each: vanilla, chocolate, strawberry ice cream
2 tablespoons each: chocolate syrup, strawberry syrup,
   butterscotch sauce   **30 ml**
Whipped cream
Maraschino cherries

+ Peel banana and slice in 2 pieces lengthwise.
+ Put 1 scoop each of vanilla, chocolate and strawberry ice cream between slices of banana.
+ Pour chocolate syrup, strawberry syrup and butterscotch sauce over scoops of ice cream.
+ Top with whipped cream and maraschino cherry.

Optional: Finely chopped nuts sprinkled over top are really great!

Variations: Try Neapolitan ice cream instead of chocolate, vanilla and strawberry.

Invent your own special ice cream and topping selections. Top with sprinkles, cinnamon candies, chocolate chips, peanut butter chips, brickle chips, M&Ms, candy bars, cookies, almond slivers and the list goes on. What will you come up with to make this a memorable dessert?

Desserts

Orange-Cream Dessert

2 cups (about 20) crushed chocolate sandwich cookies	480 ml
⅓ cup (⅔ stick) butter, melted	80 ml
1 (6 ounce) package orange gelatin mix	168 g
1½ cups boiling water	360 ml
½ gallon vanilla ice cream, softened	1.5 ml

+ In bowl, combine cookie crumbs and butter and set aside ¼ cup crumb mixture for topping. Press remaining crumb mixture into greased 9 x 13-inch (23 x 33 cm) dish.
+ In large bowl, dissolve gelatin in boiling water, cover and refrigerate for 30 minutes.
+ Stir ice cream into chilled gelatin until smooth. (Work fast.)
+ Pour gelatin-ice cream mixture over crust and sprinkle with reserved crumb mixture.
+ Freeze and remove from freezer 10 to 15 minutes before serving.

Ice Cream Dessert

19 ice cream sandwiches
1 (12 ounce) carton whipped topping, thawed   **340 g**
1 (11 ounce) jar hot fudge ice cream topping   **312 g**
1 cup salted peanuts   **240 ml**

- Cut 1 ice cream sandwich in half. Place 1 whole and 1 half sandwich along short side of ungreased 9 x 13-inch (23 x 33 cm) pan. Arrange 8 sandwiches in opposite direction in pan.
- Spread with half whipped topping. Spoon fudge topping by teaspoonfuls onto whipped topping. Sprinkle with ½ cup (120 ml) peanuts.
- Repeat layers with remaining ice cream sandwiches, whipped topping and peanuts. (Pan will be full.)
- Cover and freeze. Take out of freezer 20 minutes before serving.

Pretzel Cake

3 (7 ounce) packages white chocolate-covered pretzels, divided	3 (198 g)
⅓ cup (¾ stick) butter	80 ml
1 (8 ounce) jar chocolate ice cream topping	227 g
½ gallon chocolate ice cream	1.5 ml
⅓ cup chopped pecans	80 ml

+ Crush 1½ packages pretzels and cut in butter. Press crumb mixture into bottom of greased springform pan. Place in freezer for 1 hour.
+ Spread ice cream topping over pretzels and freeze.
+ Crush remaining pretzels and fold into softened ice cream. Spread ice cream over ice cream topping and sprinkle with chopped pecans. (Work quickly.)
+ Cover and freeze overnight before serving.

Old-Fashioned Ice Cream

2 cups half-and-half cream, divided	480 ml
¾ cup sugar	180 ml
1 cup whipping cream	240 ml
2 teaspoons vanilla extract	10 ml
2 teaspoons fresh lemon juice	10 ml

- In small saucepan over low heat, cook 1 cup (240 ml) half-and-half and sugar. Stir until sugar dissolves.
- Pour mixture into ovenproof bowl and cool to room temperature.
- Pour in remaining half-and-half, whipping cream, vanilla and lemon juice. Cover and chill at least 3 hours.
- Pour mixture into 1½-quart (1.5 L) ice cream freezer and freeze according to manufacturer's directions.
Yield: 1 quart (1 L).

Optional: Add 3 large peeled, chopped peaches or 1 pound (.5 kg) frozen peaches to ice cream. Set aside several pieces of peaches for topping and purée remaining fruit in blender. Add to ice cream before freezing.

Optional: Add 1 cup (240 ml) crushed cookies, candy bars or peppermint just before freezing. Save some of the crushed cookies, candy bars or peppermint for topping before serving.

Dark, Rich Chocolate Ice Cream

3 egg yolks	
5 ounces bittersweet chocolate	**143 g**
1¾ cups milk	**420 ml**
½ cup sugar	**120 ml**
1 cup whipping cream	**240 ml**

+ Whisk egg yolks until well beaten and set aside.
+ Chop chocolate into small pieces.
+ In medium heavy saucepan, combine milk and sugar. Cook over medium heat until mixture comes to slow boil.
+ Whisk about ½ cup (120 ml) hot milk mixture into egg yolks. Whisk egg yolk mixture back into hot milk mixture in saucepan.
+ Cook over medium low heat, whisking constantly, for 2 minutes until mixture thickens slightly. Remove from heat.
+ Add chocolate and stir until chocolate melts. Stir in cream.
+ Cool at room temperature for 30 minutes and chill about 30 minutes.
+ Freeze in ice cream maker according to manufacturer's directions.

Toffee-Ice Cream Delight

3 cups (28 cookies) crushed cream-filled chocolate sandwich cookies	710 ml
3 tablespoons butter, melted	45 ml
½ gallon French vanilla ice cream, softened, divided	1.8 L
1 (8 ounce) package milk chocolate toffee bits or	340 ml
1⅓ cups crushed chocolate-covered toffee candy bars, divided	320 ml
1 (16 ounce) jar hot fudge ice cream topping	.5 kg

- Preheat oven to 350° (176° C).
- In large bowl, combine cookie crumbs and butter. Mix well and press into bottom of ungreased 9 x 13-inch (23 x 33 cm) baking dish.
- Bake for 5 minutes. Remove from oven and cool.
- Carefully spread half ice cream over cookie crust and sprinkle with half toffee.
- Spread remaining ice cream over toffee and sprinkle with remaining toffee.
- Cover and freeze until firm. Spread fudge topping over top and keep frozen until ready to serve.

Chocolate-Marshmallow Ice Cream Pie

2 cups miniature marshmallows	480 ml
8 ounces chocolate, grated, divided	227 g
1 (5 ounce) can evaporated milk	143 g
1 (9 inch) prepared deep-dish piecrust	23 cm
1 quart vanilla ice cream, softened	1 kg

- Place marshmallows, 6 ounces (168 g) chocolate and evaporated milk in medium heavy saucepan.
- Cook and stir over medium heat until marshmallows melt. Remove from heat and cool.
- Spoon half mixture into prepared crust. Spread half ice cream over marshmallow mixture.
- Spoon remaining marshmallow mixture over ice cream and top with remaining ice cream.
- Sprinkle pie with remaining 2 ounces (57 g) grated chocolate. Cover with plastic wrap and freeze until firm.
- Let stand at room temperature for 15 minutes to soften before serving.

Layered Ice Cream Treat

2 (3 ounce) packages ladyfingers	2 (84 g)
2 pints premium chocolate-chocolate chip ice cream, softened	1 kg
1 (12 ounce) jar caramel sauce	340 g
2 pints premium vanilla ice cream, softened	1 kg
1 (12 ounce) jar fudge ice cream topping	340 g

+ Split ladyfingers and layer in bottom of 9-inch (23 cm) springform pan.
+ Stand additional ladyfingers on end with sides touching, around inside edge of pan to look like crown. Use any leftover ladyfingers to fill in bare spaces in bottom of pan. (Break them into pieces if necessary.)
+ Work quickly to spread chocolate-chocolate chip ice cream evenly over ladyfingers. Place in freezer until frozen.
+ Spread caramel sauce over chocolate-chocolate chip ice cream and freeze again.
+ Spread vanilla ice cream evenly over hardened caramel sauce and freeze.
+ Spread fudge topping over vanilla ice cream and place back in freezer until ready to serve.
+ To serve, take dessert out of pan and use sharp knife to cut slices.

Chocolate Cookie Sundae

A kids' favorite!

½ cup (1 stick) butter	120 ml
1 (19 ounce) package chocolate sandwich cookies, crushed	538 g
½ gallon vanilla ice cream, softened	1 kg
2 (12 ounce) jars fudge sauce	2 (340 g)
1 (12 ounce) carton whipped topping	340 g

+ Melt butter in 9 x 13-inch (23 x 33 cm) pan. Reserve about ½ cup (120 ml) crushed cookies for topping and mix remaining crumbs with butter to form crust. Press crumb mixture into pan.
+ Spread softened ice cream over crust (work fast) and add fudge sauce on top.
+ Top with whipped topping and sprinkle with remaining crumbs. Freeze.

Chocolate-Chocolate Gelato

6 cups milk, divided	**1.5 L**
1⅓ cups sugar	**320 ml**
12 egg yolks, beaten	
6 ounces semi-sweet chocolate, melted	**168 g**
6 ounces white baking chocolate, chopped	**168 g**

- In large saucepan over medium heat, cook 3 cups (710 ml) milk, sugar and egg yolks and stir occasionally until mixture coats metal spoon.
- Remove from heat and pour in melted chocolate. Whisk until smooth and add remaining milk. Stir to mix. Cover with plastic wrap and chill overnight.
- Stir in chopped white chocolate and freeze in 4-quart (4 L) ice cream freezer according to manufacturer's directions. Yield: 2½ quarts (2.5 L).

Tip: See meringues to use egg whites.

Macaroon Delight

12 soft coconut macaroons
1 (8 ounce) carton whipping cream, whipped   227 g
3 pints sherbet: 1 orange, 1 lime
** and 1 raspberry, softened   .5 kg**

+ Warm macaroons at 300° (148° C) for 10 minutes, break into pieces and cool.
+ Spoon macaroons into whipped cream.
+ Completely line 9 x 5-inch (23 x 13 cm) loaf pan with foil. First spread 1 pint (.5 kg) orange sherbet in loaf pan.
+ Spread half whipped cream mixture followed by lime sherbet and remaining whipped cream mixture. Raspberry sherbet goes on top.
+ Freeze overnight.
+ To serve remove from foil mold and slice.

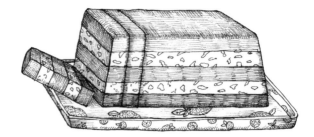

Raspberry Sherbet

1 (3 ounce) package dry raspberry gelatin mix	84 g
1 cup hot water	240 ml
1 cup orange juice	240 ml
2 tablespoons lemon juice	30 ml
¾ cup sugar	180 ml
2 cups milk	480 ml

- In large bowl, combine gelatin and hot water and stir to dissolve.
- Add orange juice, lemon juice and sugar and stir to blend. Chill until mixture thickens and becomes syrupy.
- Stir in milk and freeze until mixture becomes slushy, about 2 hours.
- Remove from freezer, beat until smooth and refreeze another several hours before serving.

Fresh Lime Sherbet

1 (3 ounce) package dry lime gelatin mix	84 g
½ cup sugar	120 ml
3 small limes	
1½ cups milk	360 ml
1 (12 ounce) can evaporated milk	384 g

+ Dissolve gelatin in 1 cup (240 ml) hot water. Stir in sugar until it dissolves.
+ Squeeze ¼ cup (60 ml) juice from limes and grate peel to yield 2 tablespoons (30 ml) zest.
+ Stir in lime juice, lime zest, milk and evaporated milk. Pour into 8-inch (20 cm) square pan.
+ Freeze for about 2 hours or until mixture becomes slushy. Remove from freezer, beat until smooth and refreeze.

Peach Sherbet

2 cups frozen sliced, unsweetened peaches, partially thawed	480 ml
½ cup plain nonfat yogurt	120 ml
2 tablespoons orange juice concentrate	30 ml
¼ cup sugar	60 ml

+ Purée peaches in food processor or blender. Add yogurt, orange juice concentrate and sugar and blend until mixture is creamy.
+ Put in square, freezer-safe pan and freeze about 2 hours until mixture becomes slushy. Remove from freezer, beat until smooth and refreeze.

Rainbow-Sherbet Delight

1 gallon vanilla ice cream, divided	3.6 L
½ gallon lime sherbet, divided	1.8 L
½ gallon orange sherbet, divided	1.8 L
1 (1.5 ounce) chocolate candy bar, shaved	45 g
2 cups chopped pecans	480 ml

+ Melt vanilla ice cream and pour 1 inch into bottom of springform pan. Place in freezer until frozen.
+ Scoop half of lime sherbet and half of orange sherbet into balls, place on top of frozen vanilla ice cream and fill pan half full. Leave space around balls and at top of pan.
+ Pour half remaining vanilla ice cream to fill spaces. Refreeze.
+ Top with shaved chocolate and pecans.
+ Repeat layer of sherbet balls and cover with remaining melted ice cream. Freeze and unmold to serve.

Cantaloupe Sherbet

1 large cantaloupe, peeled, seeded, cubed	
1 (14 ounce) can sweetened condensed milk	396 g
2 tablespoons honey	30 ml
1 tablespoon lemon juice	15 ml

- Combine all ingredients in food processor or blender. Blend until smooth.
- Freeze in ice cream maker according to manufacturer's instructions or put mixture in square, freezer-safe pan and freeze for about 2 hours or until mixture becomes slushy.
- Remove from freezer, beat until smooth and refreeze.

Icy Pineapple Freeze

1 (20 ounce) can crushed pineapple with juice	567 g
½ cup sugar	120 ml
1 (16 ounce) carton vanilla yogurt	.5 kg
½ teaspoon vanilla extract	2 ml

- In blender, purée crushed pineapple and juice until smooth.
- Pour into large bowl and stir in sugar. Let stand for 15 minutes for sugar to dissolve. Add yogurt and vanilla and mix well.
- Pour mixture into 1½-quart (1.5 ml) ice cream freezer and freeze according to manufacturer's directions.

Cranberry-Chardonnay Sorbet

*This is absolutely delicious and makes a refreshing summer dessert.
It has a beautiful dark red color and very sweet, bold taste.*

4 cups fresh or frozen cranberries	**1 L**
2 cups sugar	**480 ml**
2 cups orange juice	**480 ml**
1 cup chardonnay or other white wine	**240 ml**

+ Combine cranberries, sugar and orange juice in medium saucepan. Bring to simmer and cook until cranberries are very soft, about 5 minutes.
+ Cool mixture and purée in food processor or blender. Stir in wine. Pour into freezer-safe pan and place in freezer until slushy.
+ Remove from freezer, place in large bowl and beat until mixture is smooth. Return to freezer container and freeze until firm.

Piña Colada Sorbet

1 (15 ounce) can cream of coconut	425 ml
1 (8 ounce) can crushed pineapple with juice	227 g
3 tablespoons rum	45 ml

- Mix ¼ cup (60 ml) cold water and all ingredients in medium bowl and transfer to shallow baking dish, about 11 x 7 x 2-inch (28 x 18 x 5 cm).
- Cover and freeze, stirring every 30 minutes, until mixture freezes, about 3 hours.
- Keep covered and frozen until ready to serve. (This may be stored for several days.)

Orange Sorbet

¼ cup sugar	60 ml
⅓ cup honey	80 ml
2 cups fresh orange juice	480 ml

- Combine 1 cup (240 ml) water, sugar and honey in medium saucepan. Bring to simmer and stir occasionally until sugar dissolves.
- Let mixture simmer, uncovered, for about 10 minutes until it becomes syrupy. Cool slightly. Stir in orange juice.
- Freeze in ice cream maker according to manufacturer's instructions or place in shallow baking dish in freezer, stirring every hour, for 2 hours. Freeze until firm.

Caramel-Amaretto Dessert

1 (9 ounce) bag small chocolate-covered toffee candy bars, crumbled divided	255 g
30 caramels	
⅓ cup amaretto liqueur	80 ml
½ cup sour cream	120 ml
1 cup whipping cream	240 ml

- Reserve about ⅓ cup (80 ml) crumbled toffee bars.
- In buttered 7 x 11-inch (18 x 28 cm) dish, spread candy crumbs.
- In saucepan, melt caramels with amaretto and cool to room temperature. Stir in creams, whip until thick and pour into individual dessert dishes.
- Top with reserved candy crumbs, cover and freeze.

Grasshopper Dessert

26 chocolate sandwich cookies, crushed	
¼ cup (½ stick) butter, melted	**60 ml**
¼ cup crème de menthe liqueur	**60 ml**
2 (7 ounce) jars marshmallow cream	**2 (198 g)**
2 (8 ounce) cartons whipping cream	**2 (227 g)**

• Combine cookie crumbs and butter. Reserve about ⅓ cup (80 ml) crumbs for topping and press remaining crumbs into bottom of greased 9-inch (23 cm) springform pan.
• Gradually add crème de menthe to marshmallow cream. Beat whipping cream until very thick and fold into marshmallow mixture. Pour over crumbs.
• Sprinkle remaining crumbs on top. Freeze.

Mint Special

1 tablespoon butter	**15 ml**
20 chocolate sandwich cookies, crushed, divided	
1 pint whipping cream	**.5 g**
1¾ cups colored after-dinner mints	**420 ml**
4 cups miniature marshmallows	**1.1 L**

• Butter 9 x 11-inch (23 x 33 cm) baking dish. Reserve ½ cup (120 ml) crushed cookies and set aside. Press remaining crumbs into bottom of dish.
• In chilled medium bowl, beat whipping cream until stiff peaks form.
• Fold mints and marshmallow into whipped cream. Spread carefully over cookie crumbs in baking dish.
• Sprinkle reserved cookie crumbs over top. Chill 8 hours or overnight.

Famous Flaming Desserts

Flambé [flahm-BAY] is French for "flamed" or "flaming".
This dramatic presentation consists of sprinkling
certain foods with warmed liquor and igniting at the
dining table so guests may see the preparation.

Bananas Foster

This elegant dish was created at New Orleans' Brennan's
Restaurant in the 1950s in honor of Richard Foster, a
regular customer. Sliced bananas are quickly sautéed in
a mixture of rum, brown sugar and banana liqueur and
served with vanilla ice cream. This simplified version
omits the banana liqueur but doesn't suffer for it.

3 large bananas	
½ cup (1 stick) butter	**120 ml**
½ cup firmly packed brown sugar	**120 ml**
⅛ teaspoon cinnamon	**.5 ml**
⅓ cup rum	**80 ml**

- Peel bananas and slice in half at a diagonal. Slice each half vertically to total 12 pieces and set aside.
- Combine butter, brown sugar and cinnamon in medium saucepan over medium high heat.
- Stir until thick, about 3 to 4 minutes. Add bananas and sauté until tender, about 2 minutes. Coat them with sauce as they cook.
- Heat rum in microwave on HIGH for 30 seconds. Pour warmed rum over mixture and carefully ignite.
- Spoon mixture over bananas until flames die and immediately serve over vanilla ice cream or pound cake.

Desserts

Crêpes Suzette

This delectable dessert has a warm, buttery, orange-flavored sauce. The crêpes taste great by themselves but are much better with a scoop of premium vanilla ice cream on the side.

8 prepared dessert crêpes
2 oranges, divided
⅓ cup (⅔ stick) butter   **80 ml**
⅓ cup sugar   **80 ml**
4 ounces Grand Marnier
  (or other orange liqueur), divided   **114 g**

- Grate peel of 1 orange for zest and squeeze juice from both oranges.
- Cream butter, sugar and orange zest and place in large chaffing dish over medium-high heat.
- Cook until mixture bubbles and continue cooking and stirring occasionally until mixture begins to brown.
- Gradually add orange juice and stir after each addition.
- Stir in 2 ounces (57 g) orange liqueur and cook until mixture thickens slightly.
- (Work with 1 crêpe at a time.) Fold crêpe in half, place in orange mixture and turn to coat both sides. Use two forks to fold crêpe in half again and move to side of dish. Repeat procedure for all crêpes.
- Heat remaining liqueur in microwave on HIGH for 45 seconds and pour into dish. Do not stir and carefully ignite liqueur.
- Spoon flaming sauce over crêpes and serve. (Plan to serve two crêpes per person.)

Cherries Jubilee

If you want to impress your family and friends with a dramatic, but simple, end to a lovely meal, serve Cherries Jubilee. It is a simple 5-minute recipe, but the flame right a your table makes a lasting memory.

1 (15 ounce) can pitted dark, sweet cherries	425 g
Orange juice	
2 tablespoons cornstarch	30 ml
2 tablespoons sugar	30 ml
⅓ cup orange liqueur	80 ml

+ Drain cherries and reserve syrup. Add enough orange juice to syrup to make 1½ cups (360 ml) liquid.
+ Add about 2 tablespoons (30 ml) liquid mixture to cornstarch and stir to make a smooth paste.
+ Combine remaining syrup mixture, sugar and cornstarch paste in chafing dish. Cook and stir over medium heat until thick, about 4 minutes.
+ Add cherries to mixture and stir.
+ Heat orange liqueur in microwave on HIGH for about 1½ minutes. Pour over cherries without stirring. Ignite carefully and stir until flames subside.
+ Spoon over vanilla ice cream or brownies.

Tip: Use Kirsch or brandy instead of orange liqueur for the traditional flavoring.

Cherries Jubilee in a Flash

This is about as simple as it gets. It's
wonderful over vanilla ice cream.

1 (20 ounce) can cherry pie filling	**567 g**
¼ to ½ cup brandy	**60 - 120 ml**
Vanilla ice cream	

- Pour cherry pie filling into chafing dish or skillet. Cook and stir over medium heat until hot.
- In small saucepan, heat brandy until slightly warm. (Do not overheat.)
- Pour brandy over pie filling and carefully ignite. Gently shake pan back and forth to increase flame.
- Spoon immediately over ice cream.

> *Tip: For a non-alcoholic sauce, omit brandy. Flame by soaking 6 sugar cubes in orange extract for 5 minutes. Place soaked cubes on top of hot pie filling. Ignite cubes just before serving.*

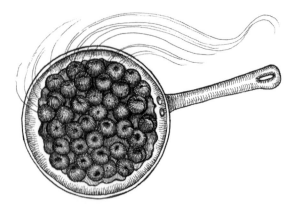

Island Volcano Flambé

3 large oranges	
1 (20 ounce) can crushed pineapple with juice	**567 g**
3 teaspoons cornstarch	**15 ml**
¼ cup rum	**60 ml**
1 quart vanilla ice cream	**1 L**

- Squeeze ½ cup (120 ml) juice from oranges and grate peel to make 1 teaspoon (5 ml) zest.
- In skillet or chafing dish, stir orange juice, orange zest and pineapple with juice over medium low heat.
- Add cornstarch and cook until mixture bubbles and thickens to sauce consistency.
- In separate saucepan, heat rum just until warm. Ignite and pour into chafing dish over pineapple mixture.
- When flames subside, spoon over ice cream.

Winter Wonder Dessert

28 chocolate-sandwich cookies, divided
2¾ cups milk   **660 ml**
3 (3.4 ounce) packages instant pistachio pudding **3 (98 g)**
1 (8 ounce) carton whipped topping   **227 g**

- Crush cookies and reserve ⅔ cup (160 ml) crumbs. Place remaining crushed cookies in 9 x 13-inch (23 x 33 cm) dish.
- In mixing bowl, combine milk and pudding mix and blend for 2 minutes or until thick. Pour over crushed cookies.
- Spread whipped topping over pistachio pudding.
- Sprinkle reserved cookies over whipped topping and chill overnight before serving.

O'Shaughnessy's Special

1 (10 ounce) pound cake loaf   **280 g**
1 (15 ounce) can crushed pineapple with juice   **425 g**
1 (3.4 ounce) box instant pistachio pudding mix   **98 g**
1 (8 ounce) carton whipped topping   **227 g**

- Slice cake horizontally into 3 equal layers.
- Combine pineapple and pudding mix and beat until mixture begins to thicken.
- Fold in whipped topping and blend well. (You may add a few drops of green food coloring if you would like the cake to be a brighter green.)
- Spread pineapple mixture on each cake layer and on top. Chill.

Twinkie Dessert

1 (10 count) box twinkies	10
4 bananas, sliced	
1 (5.1 ounce) package instant vanilla pudding mix	146 g
1 (20 ounce) can crushed pineapple, drained	567 g
1 (8 ounce) carton whipped topping	227 g

+ Slice twinkies in half lengthwise and place in buttered 9 x 13-inch (23 x 33 cm) pan cream side up.
+ Make layer of sliced bananas.
+ Prepare pudding according to package directions (use 2 cups/480 ml milk).
+ Pour pudding over bananas and add pineapple.
+ Top with whipped topping and refrigerate.
+ Cut into squares to serve.

Chiffon Torte

1 round bakery orange chiffon cake	
1 (20 ounce) can crushed pineapple with juice	567 g
1 (5.1 ounce) package instant vanilla pudding mix	148 g
1 (8 ounce) carton whipped topping	227 g

+ Slice cake horizontally into 3 equal layers.
+ In mixing bowl, combine pineapple and pudding mix and beat by hand until mixture is thick.
+ Fold in whipped topping, spread mixture on each cake layer and over top of cake.
+ Chill overnight.

Optional: Toasted almonds may be sprinkled on top of cake.

Butterscotch Finale

1 (16 ounce) carton whipping cream	.5 kg
¾ cup butterscotch ice cream topping	180 ml
1 (9 inch) prepared round angel food cake	23 cm
¾ pound toffee bars, crushed, divided	227 g

- In mixing bowl, whip cream until thick.
- Slowly add butterscotch topping and continue to beat until mixture is thick.
- Slice cake horizontally into 3 equal layers.
- Place bottom layer on cake plate, spread with 1½ cups (360 ml) whipped cream mixture and sprinkle with one-fourth crushed toffee. Repeat layers and frost top as well as sides of cake with whipped cream mixture.
- Sprinkle toffee over top of cake. Chill for at least 8 hours before serving.

Lime-Angel Dessert

1 (6 ounce) package lime gelatin mix	168 g
1 (20 ounce) can crushed pineapple with juice	567 g
1 tablespoon lime juice, 1 tablespoon sugar	15 ml
1 (8 ounce) cartons whipping cream, whipped	227 g
1 (14 ounce) prepared angel food cake	396 g

- Dissolve gelatin in 1 cup (240 ml) boiling water and mix well.
- Stir in pineapple, lime juice and sugar.
- Cool in refrigerator until mixture thickens.
- Fold in whipped cream.
- Break cake into pieces and place in 9 x 13-inch (23 x 33 cm) dish.
- Pour pineapple mixture over cake and refrigerate overnight. Cut into squares to serve.

Blueberry-Angel Dessert

1 (8 ounce) package cream cheese, softened	227 g
1 cup powdered sugar	240 ml
1 (8 ounce) carton whipped topping, thawed	227 g
1 (14 ounce) prepared bakery angel food cake	396 g
2 (20 ounce) cans blueberry pie filling	2 (567 g)

+ In large mixing bowl, beat cream cheese and powdered sugar and fold in whipped topping.
+ Tear cake into small 1 or 2-inch (5 cm) cubes and fold into cream cheese mixture.
+ Spread mixture evenly in 9 x 13-inch (23 x 33 cm) dish and top with pie filling.
+ Cover and refrigerate for at least 3 hours before cutting into squares to serve.

Strawberry-Angel Dessert

1 (6 ounce) package dry strawberry gelatin mix	168 g
2 (10 ounce) cartons frozen strawberries with juice	2 (280 g)
2 (8 ounce) carton whipping cream, whipped	2 (227 g)
1 (14 ounce) prepared bakery angel food cake	396 g

+ Dissolve gelatin in 1 cup (240 ml) boiling water and mix well.
+ Stir in strawberries and cool in refrigerator until mixture begins to thicken.
+ Fold in whipped cream.
+ Break cake into pieces and place in 9 x 13-inch (23 x 33 cm) dish.
+ Pour strawberry mixture over cake pieces and refrigerate overnight.
+ Cut into squares to serve.

Fruit Cocktail Tortillas

1 cup packed brown sugar	240 ml
2 cups (4 sticks) butter, divided	480 ml
3 packages (8 inch) flour tortillas	3 (20 cm)
4 (15 ounce) cans fruit cocktail,	
thoroughly drained	4 (425 g)

- Preheat oven to 325° (162° C).
- In small saucepan over low heat, stir brown sugar and ⅓ cup (80 ml) butter until sugar melts and mixes well.
- Use remaining butter and brush flour tortillas on both sides. (If each tortilla is not soft enough to roll without breaking, wrap 2 or 3 at a time in damp paper towels and heat for 30 seconds in microwave oven.)
- Place 2 teaspoons (10 ml) brown sugar mixture and 1 tablespoon (15 ml) drained fruit cocktail in middle of each tortilla.
- Roll each tortilla and place, seam side down, in 11 x 7 x 2-inch (28 x 18 x 5 cm) baking pan. Spread remaining sugar mixture on top.
- Bake, covered, 10 to 15 minutes or until sugar mixture bubbles.

Pavlova

3 large egg whites	
1 cup sugar	240 ml
1 teaspoon vanilla extract	5 ml
2 teaspoons white vinegar	10 ml
3 tablespoons cornstarch	45 ml

+ Preheat oven to 300° (148° C).
+ Beat egg whites until stiff and add 3 tablespoons (45 ml) COLD water.
+ Beat again and add sugar very gradually while beating.
+ Continue beating slowly and add vanilla, vinegar and cornstarch.
+ On parchment-covered baking sheet, draw 9-inch (23 cm) circle and mound mixture within circle.
+ Bake for 45 minutes. Leave in oven to cool.
+ To serve, peel paper from bottom while sliding Pavlova onto serving plate. Cover with whipped cream and top with assortment of fresh fruit such as kiwi, strawberries, blueberries, etc.

Strawberry Pavlova

5 egg whites	
1¾ cup sugar, divided	**420 ml**
1 teaspoon vinegar	**5 ml**
1½ cups whipping cream	**360 ml**
2 pints strawberries, washed, hulled, halved	**1 kg**

+ Preheat oven to 250° (121° C).
+ Line baking sheet with foil or parchment paper. Use bowl or round baking dish as template and draw 10-inch (25 cm) wide circle on foil or paper. Set aside.
+ Beat egg whites at high speed until soft peaks form.
+ Gradually add 1½ (360 ml) cups sugar and continue to beat until mixture is white and glossy with soft peaks, about 10 minutes.
+ Add vinegar and beat at high speed for another 5 minutes.
+ With small, flexible spatula, spread meringue mixture inside circle on baking sheet. Keep sides straight and top as flat as possible.
+ Draw spatula up sides of meringue circle to form "ribs". (This will give a finished look and add strength once meringue bakes.)
+ Bake for 1 hour. Turn oven off and leave pavlova in oven for another 2 hours.
+ When ready to assemble, carefully remove meringue base from foil or paper and place on serving plate.
+ Beat whipping cream with remaining ½ cup (120 ml) sugar until soft peaks form and spread whipped cream evenly over surface of meringue base.
+ Arrange strawberries attractively on top and serve.

Chocolate-Cherry Pavlova

*You can alter the flavor of basic Pavlova with
liqueur and fruit to create a dessert that is just as
delicious and with a personality all its own.*

5 egg whites	
1¾ cups sugar, divided	420 ml
1 teaspoon vinegar	5 ml
1½ cups whipping cream	360 ml
¼ cup crème de cacao liqueur	60 ml
1 (15 ounce) can cherries, well drained	425 ml
1 (3.5 ounce) chocolate bar, grated	100 g

+ Preheat oven to 250° (121° C).
+ Prepare baking sheet by lining with foil or parchment paper. Use bowl and draw 10-inch (25 cm) wide circle on foil or paper. Set aside.
+ Beat egg whites at high speed until soft peaks form.
+ Gradually add 1½ cups (360 ml) sugar and continue to beat until mixture is white and glossy with soft peaks, about 10 minutes. Add vinegar and beat at high speed for another 5 minutes.
+ With small, spatula, spread meringue mixture inside circle on baking sheet. Keep sides straight and top as flat as possible.
+ Draw spatula up sides of meringue circle to form "ribs". (This will strength once meringue is baked.)
+ Bake for 1 hour. Turn over off and leave pavlova in oven for another 2 hours.
+ When ready to assemble, carefully remove meringue base from foil or paper and place on serving plate.
+ Beat whipping cream with remaining ½ cup (120 ml) sugar and crème de cacao until soft peaks form and spread whipped cream over surface of meringue base.
+ Arrange cherries attractively on top and garnish with grated chocolate.

Best Pavlova
with Creamy Topping

10 large egg whites
1 tablespoon white vinegar   15 ml
2¼ cups sugar   540 ml
2½ tablespoons cornstarch   600 ml

Topping:
1 pint whipping cream   .5 kg
¾ cup sugar   180 ml
1 teaspoon vanilla extract   5 ml
Fresh fruits

- Preheat oven to 275° (135° C).
- With mixer, beat egg whites on low speed. (Make sure there is absolutely no yolk in the egg whites.)
- Add vinegar and a pinch of salt while mixing on low.
- Combine 2¼ cups (540 ml) sugar and cornstarch, add mixture gradually to egg whites and beat on low until well incorporated. Turn speed to high and beat for 5 minutes or until stiff peaks form.
- Spread greased parchment paper on baking sheet and spoon egg mixture onto paper. Form mixture into 10-inch (25 cm) circle and flatten top. Place baking sheet in oven for 10 minutes or until shell forms.
- Reduce heat to 240° (115° C) and continue cooking about 1 hour or until meringue begins to crack. (Do not brown.) Cool meringue completely.
- To serve, beat whipping cream and gradually add ¾ cup (180 ml) sugar and vanilla. Beat until stiff peaks form.
- Spread whipped cream mixture over meringue and place slices of fresh peaches, mango, kiwi, banana or choice of fruit. (Do not top meringue with whipped cream and fruit until just before serving.)

Candies

Stained Glass Fudge

1 (12 ounce) package chocolate chips	340 g
½ cup (1 stick) butter	120 ml
1 cup coarsely chopped pecans or walnuts	240 ml
1 (10 ounce) bag miniature	
colored marshmallows	280 g
½ cup flaked coconut	120 ml

- Melt chocolate and butter in top of double boiler over simmering water and stir constantly until mixture is smooth. Remove from heat and cool slightly.
- Stir in nuts and marshmallows.
- Divide mixture in half and shape each into 2-inch (5 cm) wide log.
- Roll logs in coconut and wrap each in plastic wrap or foil. Chill for several hours or overnight.
- Slice each log into pieces about ⅓-inch (.8 cm) thick.

Easy, Fast Fudge

1 (14 ounce) can sweetened condensed milk	396 g
3 cups semi-sweet or milk chocolate chips	710 ml
Pinch salt	
1 teaspoon vanilla extract	5 ml

- Combine sweetened condensed milk, chocolate chips and salt in medium saucepan over medium low heat. Stir constantly until chocolate melts.
- Remove from heat and stir in vanilla.
- Spread in buttered 8 x 8-inch (20 x 20 cm) pan and cool.

Microwave Chocolate Fudge

2 (10 ounce) packages milk chocolate chips	2 (280 g)
1 (14 ounce) can sweetened condensed milk	396 g
¼ cup (½ stick) butter, sliced	60 ml
½ cup chopped pecans	120 ml

- Combine chocolate chips, sweetened condensed milk and butter in a microwave-safe bowl.
- Microwave on MEDIUM for 4 to 5 minutes or until chocolate melts. Stir several times.
- Stir in pecans and pour into greased 9-inch (23 cm) square pan.
- Chill several hours and cut into squares. Store in refrigerator.

Diamond Fudge

1 (6 ounce) package semi-sweet chocolate morsels	168 g
1 cup creamy peanut butter	240 ml
½ cup (1 stick) butter	120 ml
1 cup powdered sugar	240 ml

- Combine morsels, peanut butter and butter in saucepan over low heat. Stir constantly, just until mixture melts and is smooth.
- Remove from heat, add powdered sugar and stir until smooth.
- Spoon into buttered 8-inch (20 cm) square pan and chill until firm.
- Let stand 10 minutes at room temperature before cutting into squares and store in refrigerator.

Raisin Fudge

1 (12 ounce) package semi-sweet chocolate chips	340 g
1 cup chunky peanut butter	240 ml
3 cups miniature marshmallows	710 ml
¾ cup raisins	180 ml

+ In saucepan melt chocolate chips and peanut butter over medium-low heat.
+ Fold in marshmallows and raisins and stir until marshmallows melt.
+ Pour into 7 x 11-inch (18 x 28 cm) pan.
+ Chill until firm. Cut into squares and store in cool spot.

Peanut Butter Fudge

1 (12 ounce) jar chunky peanut butter	340 g
1 (12 ounce) package milk chocolate chips	340 g
1 (14 ounce) can sweetened condensed milk	396 g
1 cup chopped pecans	240 ml

+ Melt peanut butter and chocolate chips.
+ Add sweetened condensed milk and heat.
+ Add pecans and mix well.
+ Pour into buttered 9 x 9-inch (23 x 23 cm) dish.

Creamy Peanut Butter Fudge

3 cups sugar	710 g
¾ cup (1½ sticks) butter	180 ml
⅔ cup evaporated milk	160 ml
1 (10 ounce) package peanut butter-flavored morsels	280 g
1 (7 ounce) jar marshmallow cream	198 g
1 teaspoon vanilla extract	5 ml

+ Combine sugar, butter and evaporated milk in large saucepan.
+ Bring to boil over medium heat and stir constantly. Cover and cook 3 minutes without stirring.
+ Uncover and boil 5 minutes (do not stir).
+ Remove from heat, add morsels and stir until morsels melt.
+ Stir in marshmallow cream and vanilla.
+ Pour into buttered 9 x 13-inch (23 x 33 cm) pan and place in freezer for 10 minutes.

White Chocolate Fudge

*This is a little different slant to fudge -
really creamy and really good!*

1 (8 ounce) package cream cheese, softened	227 g
4 cups powdered sugar	1.1 L
1½ teaspoons vanilla extract	340 g
12 ounces almond bark, melted	180 ml
¾ cup chopped pecans	

+ Beat cream cheese at medium speed with mixer until smooth, gradually add sugar and vanilla and beat well.
+ Stir in melted almond bark and pecans and spread into buttered 8-inch (20 cm) square pan.
+ Refrigerate until firm and cut into small squares.

Snowy Almond Fudge

1 (10 ounce) package premier white chocolate chips	280 g
⅔ cup sweetened condensed milk	160 ml
1½ cups chopped, slivered almonds, toasted	360 ml
½ teaspoon vanilla extract	2 ml

+ Line bottom and sides of 8 x 8-inch (20 x 20 cm) pan with foil and set aside.
+ In medium saucepan, melt white chocolate chips with sweetened condensed milk over very low heat and stir constantly.
+ Remove from heat, stir in almonds and vanilla and mix well.
+ Pour into foil-lined pan and cover.
+ Chill for several hours until firm. Remove from refrigerator and lift fudge from pan with foil.
+ Remove foil and cut into squares.

Quick Chocolate Bites

This is a 5-minute solution for unhappy kids.

2 cups semi-sweet or milk chocolate chips	480 ml
1 tablespoon butter	15 ml
½ cup raisins	120 ml
½ cup chopped pecans, toasted	120 ml

- Combine chocolate chips and butter in top of double boiler over simmering water. Stir frequently until chocolate melts and mixture is smooth.
- Remove from heat and stir in raisins and pecans.
- Drop by heaping teaspoonfuls onto wax paper or foil. Chill until ready to serve.

Tip: To toast pecans, spread out on baking sheet and cook at 350° (176° C) for about 5 minutes until nuts are light brown.

Chocolate-Peanut Clusters

1 cup semi-sweet chocolate chips	240 ml
½ cup premier white chocolate chips	120 ml
1 tablespoon shortening	15 ml
1 (11 ounce) package lightly salted peanuts, divided	312 g

+ Microwave all chocolate chips and shortening on HIGH for 1 to 2 minutes or until chips melt.
+ Stir until chips blend and mixture is smooth.
+ Set aside ¼ cup (60 ml) peanuts for topping.
+ Pour remaining peanuts into chocolate mixture and mix well.
+ Drop by teaspoonfuls into 1-inch (2.5 cm) clusters on baking sheet. Put remaining peanuts on top of each cluster.
+ Chill until clusters are firm and store in airtight container. Yield: 2½ to 3 dozen clusters.

Creole Pralines

3 cups sugar	710 ml
1 teaspoon vinegar	5 ml
1 tablespoon butter	15 ml
3 cups chopped pecans	710 ml

+ Combine sugar, 1 cup (240 ml) water and vinegar and cook to soft-ball stage or when candy thermometer reaches 236° (115° C).
+ Stir in butter and pecans. Remove from heat and beat until mixture is slightly thick.
+ Drop by teaspoonfuls onto wax paper. Cool completely.

Crunchy Pecan Bites

½ cup (1 stick) butter, softened	120 ml
2 tablespoons light corn syrup	30 ml
½ cup sugar	120 ml
¾ cup chopped pecans	180 ml
1 (12 ounce) package milk chocolate chips	340 ml

+ Line 9-inch (23 cm) square pan with aluminum foil and coat foil with non-stick spray.
+ In heavy saucepan over medium heat, melt butter and stir in corn syrup and sugar. Stir constantly until sugar dissolves.
+ Add pecans and stir until mixture begins to thicken and turn golden brown.
+ Pour chocolate chips evenly over bottom of prepared pan. Pour butter mixture over chocolate chips and spread evenly.
+ Cool several hours to set or chill in refrigerator.
+ Remove from foil and break into pieces.

Cracker Candy Bites

2¾ cups round buttery crackers	660 ml
¾ cup (1½ sticks) butter	180 ml
2 cups packed brown sugar	480 ml
1 (12 ounce) package milk chocolate chips	340 g

+ Preheat oven to 350° (176° C).
+ Place crackers in greased 9 x 13-inch (23 x 33 cm) baking dish.
+ In saucepan, combine butter and brown sugar and bring to boil. Boil 3 minutes, stir constantly and pour mixture over crackers.
+ Bake for 5 minutes and TURN OVEN OFF.
+ Sprinkle chocolate chips over cracker mixture. Return to oven and let stand about 5 minutes or until chocolate melts.
+ Remove from oven and spread chocolate evenly over cracker mixture. Cool and break into pieces.

Sugar Plum Candy

1¼ pounds vanilla-flavored almond bark, chopped	567 g
1½ cups miniature red and green marshmallows	360 ml
1½ cups peanut butter cereal	360 ml
1½ cups crispy rice cereal	360 ml
1½ cups mixed nuts	360 ml

+ In double boiler on low heat, melt almond bark.
+ Place marshmallows, cereals and nuts in large bowl, pour melted bark over mixture and stir to coat.
+ Drop mixture by teaspoonfuls onto wax paper-lined baking sheet.
+ Let stand until set and store in airtight container.

Pecan Toffee

This delightful candy is very easy to make.

2 tablespoons (¼ stick) plus 1 cup (2 sticks) butter	30 ml; 240 ml
1 cup firmly packed brown sugar	240 ml
1 cup coarsely chopped pecans	240 ml
2 (3.5 ounce) premium dark or milk chocolate bars	2 (100 g)

+ Use 2 tablespoons (30 ml) butter to grease 9 x 13-inch (23 x 33 cm) baking dish and large saucepan.
+ Place remaining 1 cup (240 ml) butter in saucepan and melt over medium high heat. Stir in brown sugar and bring to boil.
+ Boil sugar mixture for 12 minutes, stirring constantly and occasionally washing down sides of pan with wet pastry brush.
+ Remove pan from heat and quickly stir in pecans.
+ Pour toffee mixture into prepared baking dish and use buttered spatula to spread evenly.
+ Place chocolate bars on top of toffee and melt. When melted, spread chocolate evenly over surface.
+ Cool and cut into pieces.

Cashew Crunch

1 cup sugar	240 ml
1 cup (2 sticks) butter	240 ml
1 tablespoon light corn syrup	15 ml
1½ cups salted cashew pieces	360 ml

- In medium saucepan over medium heat, melt sugar, butter and corn syrup. Stir frequently.
- Cook until candy thermometer reaches 300° (148° C), about 25 to 30 minutes.
- Pour into large, wax paper-lined baking pan and spread to about ¼-inch (.6 cm) thickness.
- Sprinkle cashew pieces over top and press down lightly.
- Cool thoroughly and break into pieces.

Tip: If no candy thermometer is available, pour several drops sugar mixture into ice water. If brittle strands form, candy is ready.

Chocolate Toffee

1 cup sugar	240 ml
1 cup (2 sticks) butter	240 ml
1 (6 ounce) package chocolate chips	168 g
1 cup chopped pecans	240 ml

- In heavy saucepan, combine sugar and butter. Cook until candy reaches hard-crack stage and pour onto greased baking sheet.
- Melt chocolate in double boiler and spread over toffee.
- Sprinkle with pecans and press pecans into chocolate.
- Chill until chocolate sets and break into pieces.

Almond-Butter Toffee

1 cup sugar	240 ml
1 cup (2 sticks) butter	240 ml
1 (6 ounce) package semi-sweet chocolate chips	168 g
¼ cup sliced almonds	60 ml

- In medium saucepan over medium heat, melt sugar and butter and stir frequently.
- Cook until candy thermometer reaches 300° (148° C), about 25 to 30 minutes.
- Pour into large, wax paper-lined baking pan and spread to about ¼-inch (.6 cm) thickness.
- Sprinkle chocolate chips over candy and spread evenly. Let stand for at least 5 minutes.
- Sprinkle with almonds and press down lightly.
- Cool thoroughly and break into pieces.

Tip: If no candy thermometer is available, pour several drops sugar mixture into ice water. If brittle strands form, candy is ready.

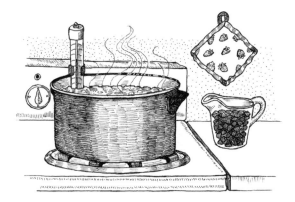

Almond Caramels

12 graham cracker squares	
¾ cup packed brown sugar	180 ml
¾ cup (1½ sticks) butter	180 ml
1 (6 ounce) package premium	
semi-sweet chocolate chips	168 g
1 cup slivered almonds	240 ml

+ Lay graham crackers in bottom of foil-lined 15 x 10-inch (35 x 25 cm) jellyroll pan.
+ In medium saucepan over medium heat, melt butter and brown sugar, stirring frequently, until sugar dissolves.
+ Bring sugar mixture to full boil and stir continuously for about 5 minutes.
+ Pour mixture over graham crackers and spread to coat crackers.
+ Cover with chocolate chips and let stand 1 minute. Spread chocolate chips in swirling motion.
+ Sprinkle almonds over top and press slivers into chocolate.
+ Cool thoroughly and break into pieces.

Microwave Pecan Brittle

*This candy is very easy, and it does not
require a candy thermometer!*

1 cup sugar	240 ml
½ cup light corn syrup	120 ml
1 cup pecan halves or pieces	240 ml
1 teaspoon butter	5 ml
1 teaspoon baking soda	5 ml

+ Put sugar and corn syrup in large microwave-safe bowl. Cook on HIGH for 4 minutes.
+ Stir in pecans and cook on HIGH for another 4 minutes.
+ Stir in butter and mix well. Return to microwave and cook on HIGH for 2 minutes.
+ Add baking soda and stir until foamy.
+ Grease baking sheet or shallow-rimmed baking pan. Spread mixture on sheet or in pan and cool for 30 minutes. Break into pieces.

> *Tip: For additional flavor, you may add
> ¼ teaspoon (1 ml) cinnamon with the sugar and corn
> syrup and 1 teaspoon (5 ml) vanilla extract with the
> butter.*

Walnut Maples

*This is a take-off from the favorite peanut
brittle. It is really a nice change.*

1 cup packed brown sugar	**240 ml**
¾ cup maple syrup	**180 ml**
¼ cup (½ stick) butter	**60 ml**
1 cup salted walnuts	**240 ml**
½ teaspoon baking soda	**2 ml**

+ In medium saucepan over medium heat, stir brown sugar and syrup until sugar dissolves.
  (Stir frequently so sugar does not burn.)
+ Bring sugar-syrup mixture to boil and continue to stir, about 5 to 8 minutes.
+ Add butter to mixture and continue cooking until temperature on candy thermometer reaches 300° (148° C) about 15 minutes.
+ Remove from heat and stir in walnuts and baking soda. Pour mixture onto large, buttered baking sheet and spread to about ¼-inch (.6 cm) thickness.
+ Cool completely and break into pieces.

> *Tip: If you do not have a candy thermometer, pour
> a few drops of sugar mixture into ice water. If hard,
> brittle strands form, candy is ready for walnuts and
> baking soda.*

Tiger Butter

1 pound white chocolate or almond bark	.5 kg
½ cup chunky peanut butter	120 ml
1 cup semi-sweet chocolate morsels	240 ml

- Line 15 x 10-inch (35 x 25 cm) jellyroll pan with wax paper.
- Heat white chocolate in microwave-safe bowl on HIGH for 1 to 2 minutes or until it melts.
- Stir until smooth, add peanut butter and microwave on HIGH until it melts.
- Stir again until smooth and spread mixture evenly into prepared pan.
- In another microwave-safe bowl, melt chocolate morsels on HIGH.
- Pour chocolate over peanut butter mixture and swirl through with knife until you get desired effect.
- Refrigerate several hours until firm and break into pieces.

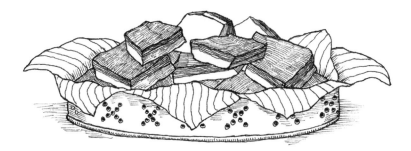

Sweet Crispies

1 (6 ounce) package semi-sweet chocolate chips	168 g
¾ cup crunchy peanut butter	180 ml
6 cups bite-size crispy corn and wheat cereal	1.5 L
1½ cups powdered sugar	360 ml

- Place chocolate chips in microwave-safe bowl, melt in microwave and stir two times.
- Stir peanut butter into chocolate and mix well.
- Gently stir in cereal and mix until it coats well.
- Place powdered sugar in large, resealable plastic bag and add cereal mixture. Seal and gently toss until cereal coats well.
- Store in airtight container in refrigerator.

Macadamia Candy

2 (3 ounce) jars macadamia nuts	2 (84 g)
1 (20 ounce) package white almond bark	567 g
¾ cup flaked coconut	180 ml

- Heat dry skillet and toast nuts until light golden brown. (Some brands of macadamia nuts are already toasted.) Set aside.
- In double boiler, melt 12 squares almond bark.
- As soon as almond bark melts, pour in macadamia nuts and coconut and stir well.
- Place wax paper on baking sheet, pour candy on wax paper and spread out.
- Chill for 30 minutes to set and break into pieces.

Nut Truffles

8 ounces semi-sweet chocolate, chopped	227 g
½ cup plus 2 tablespoons whipping cream	120 ml
1 tablespoon brandy	15 ml
6 tablespoons ground, toasted pecans	90 ml
⅓ cup cocoa powder	80 ml

+ Place chocolate in medium bowl.
+ Bring cream to simmer in small saucepan and pour over chocolate. Let stand for 2 minutes.
+ Whisk until smooth and mix in brandy. Cool completely, about 30 minutes, and stir occasionally.
+ With mixer, beat chocolate mixture until fluffy and lighter in color, about 4 minutes. Mix in pecans.
+ Cover and chill mixture until firm, about 2 hours.
+ Line baking sheet with wax paper.
+ Place cocoa powder in another bowl.
+ Use hands or melon baller to shape chocolate into balls about 1 inch wide. Roll each ball in cocoa to coat.
+ Cover and chill until firm.

Chocolate Truffles

¾ cup (1½ sticks) butter	180 ml
¾ cup cocoa	180 ml
1 (14 ounce) can sweetened condensed milk	396 g
3 tablespoons rum	45 ml
1 cup finely chopped pecans, divided	240 ml

- Melt butter in small saucepan and stir in cocoa until smooth. (Make sure all lumps are gone.)
- Stir constantly while slowly adding sweetened condensed milk.
- Continue to stir and cook mixture until it thickens and is smooth and shiny, about 5 minutes.
- Remove from heat and stir in rum and ¾ cup (180 ml) pecans.
- Pour into baking pan and chill for several hours until mixture is firm enough to shape.
- Remove mixture from pan by tablespoons and shape into 1-inch (2.5 cm) balls.
- Roll in remaining chopped pecans, put on plate and chill several more hours before serving.

Sauces

Easy Chocolate Sauce

½ cup whipping cream	120 ml
3 (1 ounce) squares semi-sweet baking chocolate	3 (28 g)

+ Combine whipping cream and chocolate in small saucepan.
+ Cook over low heat, stirring constantly, until chocolate melts and mixture is smooth and slightly thick.
+ Remove from heat and cool to room temperature. (If not used immediately, place in covered container and chill until ready to use.) Warm slightly in microwave if necessary before using. Yield: about ¾ cup (180 ml).

Hot Fudge Sauce

2 cups chocolate chips	480 ml
½ cup half-and-half cream	120 ml
½ teaspoon vanilla extract	2 ml

+ Combine chocolate chips and half-and-half in small saucepan over very low heat.
+ Stir constantly until chocolate melts and mixture is smooth.
+ Remove from heat and stir in vanilla. Serve warm and keep remaining sauce chilled.
+ When ready to use again, warm slightly in microwave and stir every 30 seconds until sauce can be poured.

Caramel Sauce

¼ cup sugar	60 ml
½ cup whipping cream	120 ml

- Bring sugar and 3 tablespoons (45 ml) water to boil and stir frequently until sugar dissolves.
- Simmer for about 10 minutes and swirl pan occasionally until sugar mixture is deep amber color.
- Remove from heat and quickly whisk in cream. (Mixture will bubble furiously.)
- Return to medium heat, cook and stir until mixture thickens and lumps of caramel melt. Remove from heat and cool.

Sunny Pineapple Sauce

1 (20 ounce) can pineapple pie filling	567 g
¼ cup lemon juice	60 ml
¼ cup sugar	60 ml
6 whole cloves	

- In medium saucepan over medium heat, combine all ingredients.
- Simmer for 10 minutes and remove cloves. Serve over ice cream or pound cake.

Boysenberry Sauce

1 (16 ounce) bag frozen, unsweetened	
boysenberries, thawed	**.5 kg**
½ cup sugar	**120 ml**
1 tablespoon lemon juice	**15 ml**
1 tablespoon cornstarch	**15 ml**

+ Place boysenberries, sugar and lemon juice in small, heavy saucepan. Cook and stir over medium heat to soften berries and release juice.
+ Strain mixture into small bowl and crush berries with back of spoon to strain out solids. Discard solids and pour juice back into saucepan.
+ Remove 2 tablespoons (30 ml) juice and mix with cornstarch to make paste. Stir paste into juice.
+ Cook and stir over medium heat until sauce thickens, about 4 to 5 minutes. Cover and chill until ready to serve. Yield: about 1 cup (240 ml).

Raspberry Sauce

*Serve this homemade raspberry sauce over ice cream,
cake or pudding, or put it in a syrup dispenser and
serve it on pancakes and waffles. It is wonderful!*

1 (12 ounce) bag frozen, sweetened raspberries, thawed	340 g
¼ cup orange juice, divided	60 ml
1 tablespoon cornstarch	15 ml
¼ cup sugar	60 ml

+ Purée raspberries in food processor or blender. Strain
  seeds and solids, discard contents of strainer and put
  purée in medium saucepan.
+ Dissolve cornstarch in small amount of orange juice and
  stir until smooth. Add cornstarch mixture to purée in
  pan with remaining orange juice and sugar.
+ Bring to boil over medium heat and cook, stirring
  constantly, for 1 to 2 minutes until sauce thickens.
  Remove from heat and cool. Yield: about 1 cup (240 ml).

Creamy Fruit Topping

Use this tasty topping as an accompaniment for different fruits. Consider making a fruit tray with raspberries, strawberries and pineapple and serve the topping as a dip.

1 pint whipping cream	**.5 kg**
1 cup sugar	**240 ml**
1 (.25 ounce) packet unflavored gelatin mix	**.7 g**
1 pint sour cream	**.5 kg**
1 teaspoon vanilla extract	**5 ml**

+ In medium saucepan, heat cream, sugar and gelatin until gelatin dissolves.
+ Remove mixture from heat and cool to lukewarm. Chill until mixture begins to set.
+ Fold in sour cream and vanilla and chill until ready to serve. Serve with fresh sliced fruit.

Pick Your Fruit—Here's the Dressing

½ cup mayonnaise	**120 ml**
½ cup sour cream	**120 ml**
½ cup powdered sugar	**120 ml**
1 teaspoon lemon juice	**5 ml**
½ teaspoon ground cinnamon	**2 ml**

+ In bowl, combine mayonnaise and sour cream and mix well.
+ Stir in powdered sugar, lemon juice and cinnamon until they blend well.

This dressing is wonderful over a medley of fresh pineapple, kiwi, strawberries, pears, melon, etc.

266

Hot Spiced Apple Topping

2 tablespoons (¼ stick) butter	30 ml
2 tablespoons brown sugar	30 ml
½ teaspoon apple pie spice or cinnamon	2 ml
1 (20 ounce) can apple pie filling	567 g
½ cup chopped walnuts, toasted	120 ml

+ In medium saucepan, melt butter and stir in brown sugar, apple pie spice and pie filling.
+ Bring to boil, remove from heat and stir in walnuts. Serve warm over ice cream or crêpes.

Island-Pineapple Sauce

1 (20 ounce) can pineapple pie filling	567 g
¼ cup curacao or orange liqueur	60 ml
1 tablespoon lemon juice	15 ml
1 tablespoon orange zest	15 ml

+ In small saucepan over medium heat, combine all ingredients.
+ Bring to boil and stir constantly. Serve over ice cream or pound cake.

Delicious Lemon Sauce for Pound Cake

1¼ cups Marzetti slaw dressing	300 ml
1 (8 ounce) package cream cheese, softened	227 g
¼ cup lemon juice	60 ml
¼ cup half-and-half cream	60 ml
1½ cups powdered sugar	360 ml

+ With mixer, beat dressing and cream cheese until creamy.
+ Add lemon juice, half-and-half and powdered sugar and continue beating until creamy.
+ Spoon sauce over pieces of pound cake. (It is also good over apple pie or spice cake.)

Whipped Cream

1 cup whipping cream	240 ml
4 tablespoons sugar	60 ml
2 teaspoons vanilla extract	10 ml

+ In medium bowl, beat cream on medium low speed for about 30 seconds.
+ Increase speed to medium high and slowly add sugar and vanilla.
+ Continue to beat until soft peaks form.

Whiskey Cream

Try this with pecan pie!

2 cups whipping cream	480 ml
1 cup honey	240 ml
½ cup whiskey	120 ml

+ In well chilled, medium bowl, beat cream until stiff peaks form.
+ In separate bowl, combine honey with whiskey and fold mixture gently into whipped cream. Cover and chill for several hours.

Amaretto Sauce for Pound Cake

1 (3.4 ounce) package French vanilla pudding mix (not instant)	98 g
1 cup milk	240 ml
1 (8 ounce) carton whipping cream, whipped	227 g
¼ cup amaretto liqueur	60 ml

+ Cook pudding with milk according to package directions.
+ Cover and cool to room temperature.
+ With wire whisk, stir in whipped cream and amaretto. Pour over pound cake (or vanilla ice cream).

Warm Walnut Sauce

1 cup sugar	240 ml
1 teaspoon fresh lemon juice	5 ml
⅓ cup water	80 ml
½ cup chopped walnuts	120 ml
½ cup whipping cream	120 ml

+ In medium saucepan, stir sugar, lemon juice and water and cook over medium heat, stirring constantly, until sugar dissolves.
+ Over medium-high heat, continue to cook and stir until mixture turns an amber color.
+ Add walnuts and continue to cook and stir for about 1 minute.
+ Remove from heat and slowly pour in cream while stirring. Continue to stir until sauce blends well and is slightly thick. Pour over ice cream, cake or brownies.

Rum Sauce

This delightful, buttery caramel sauce is lightly flavored with rum and goes well with a variety of fruits and desserts. Serve it warm over apple or peach cobbler, pound cake or ice cream.

6 tablespoons (¾ stick) butter	90 ml
½ cup firmly packed light brown sugar	120 ml
3 tablespoons whipping cream	45 ml
1 tablespoon light rum	15 ml

+ Melt butter in medium saucepan over medium heat. Stir in brown sugar and cook, stirring frequently, until mixture is thick and bubbly, about 5 minutes.
+ Add cream 1 tablespoon (15 ml) at a time and stir well after each addition.
+ Stir and cook until sugar dissolves and mixture is smooth, about 3 minutes. Stir in rum and cook about 1 more minute.
+ Remove from heat and serve warm.

Peanutty Ice Cream Crunch

Peanut Butter Sauce:

1 cup peanut butter chips	240 ml
⅓ cup milk	80 ml
¼ cup whipping cream	60 ml
¼ teaspoon vanilla extract	1 ml

+ In medium saucepan over low heat, melt peanut butter chips with milk and whipping cream and stir constantly until mixture is smooth.
+ Remove from heat and stir in vanilla. Cool to room temperature.

Coconut Crunch:

½ cup flaked coconut	120 ml
½ cup chopped nuts	120 ml
1 tablespoon butter	15 ml

+ Preheat oven to 300° (148° C).
+ Combine coconut, nuts and butter in small baking dish. Toast in oven 6 to 8 minutes and stir occasionally. (Watch closely so mixture does not burn.)
+ Place 1 scoop ice cream in each of 4 dessert dishes.
+ Spoon Peanut Butter Sauce over top and sprinkle with Coconut Crunch.

Candied-Almond Topping

This easy candied-almond recipe gives you a nice alternative to plain nuts as topping for ice cream and other desserts.

⅓ cup sugar	**80 ml**
½ cup slivered almonds, toasted	**120 ml**

+ Line baking sheet with aluminum foil. Bring 2 tablespoons (30 ml) water and sugar to boil in small, heavy saucepan.
+ Without stirring, cook over medium-high heat until mixture becomes deep amber color, about 10 minutes. Occasionally wash down sides of pan with wet pastry brush.
+ Remove from heat and stir in almonds. Quickly spread mixture on prepared baking sheet.
+ Cool to harden, break into small pieces and store in airtight container.

Tip: To toast the almonds, place in single layer on baking sheet and bake at 350° (176° C) until golden brown, about 5 minutes. Remove from oven and cool.

Old Southern Praline Sauce

Great poured over pound cake!

2 eggs	
1 (16 ounce) box light brown sugar	.5 kg
2 tablespoons flour	30 ml
½ cup (1 stick) butter	120 ml
1 teaspoon vanilla extract	5 ml
1½ cups chopped pecans	360 ml

+ Beat eggs, combine sugar and flour and mix.
+ In skillet, melt butter, stir in brown sugar mixture and stir constantly.
+ Remove from heat and stir in vanilla and pecans.

Toffee Crunch

½ cup sugar	120 ml
1½ teaspoons light corn syrup	7 ml
6 tablespoons (¾ stick) butter	90 ml
2 tablespoons water	30 ml

+ Lightly grease 9 x 13-inch (233 x 33 cm) baking pan. In small saucepan, combine all ingredients.
+ Over medium-high heat, bring to boil and cook, stirring constantly, until sugar dissolves.
+ Continue to boil without stirring until temperature reaches 300° (148° C) on candy thermometer and mixture turns golden brown.
+ Pour mixture onto baking sheet to cool. When toffee is cool and hard, break into small pieces and place over ice cream, cake or brownies.

Index

COOKBOOKS PUBLISHED BY
COOKBOOK RESOURCES, LLC

The Ultimate Cooking With 4 Ingredients
Easy Cooking With 5 Ingredients
The Best of Cooking With 3 Ingredients
Easy Gourmet-Style Cooking With 5 Ingredients
Gourmet Cooking With 5 Ingredients
Healthy Cooking With 4 Ingredients
Diabetic Cooking With 4 Ingredients
Easy Dessert Cooking With 5 Ingredients
4-Ingredient Recipes And 30-Minute Meals
Easy Slow-Cooker Cookbook
Quick Fixes With Cake Mixes
Casseroles To The Rescue
Kitchen Keepsakes/More Kitchen Keepsakes
Old-Fashioned Cookies
Grandmother's Cookies
Mother's Recipes
Recipe Keepsakes
Cookie Dough Secrets
Gifts For The Cookie Jar
All New Gifts For The Cookie Jar
Muffins In A Jar
Brownies In A Jar
Gifts n a Pickle Jar
Cookie Jar Magic
Quilters' Cooking Companion
Miss Sadie's Southern Cooking
Classic Tex-Mex and Texas Cooking
Classic Southwest Cooking
Bake Sale Bestsellers
Easy Desserts
The Great Canadian Cookbook
The Best of Lone Star Legacy Cookbook
Lone Star Legacy
Lone Star Legacy II
Cookbook 25 Years
Pass The Plate
Authorized Texas Ranger Cookbook
Texas Longhorn Cookbook
Trophy Hunters' Wild Game Cookbook
Mealtimes and Memories
Holiday Recipes
Homecoming
Little Taste of Texas
Little Taste of Texas II
Texas Peppers
Southwest Sizzler
Southwest Ole
Class Treats
Leaving Home

To Order: *To order Easy Desserts*

Please send_____ hardcover copies @ $19.95 (U.S.) each $ _____

Texas residents add sales tax @ $1.60 each $ _____

Please send_____ paperback copies @ $16.95 (U.S.) each $_____

Texas residents add sales tax @ $1.34 each $_____

Plus postage/handling @ $6.00 (1st copy) $ _____

$1.00 (each additional copy) $ _____

Check or Credit Card (Canada-credit card only) **Total** $ _____

Charge to: ❑ MasterCard.   or   ❑ VISA

Account # _____

Expiration Date _____

Signature_____

| Mail or Call: |
| Cookbook Resources |
| 541 Doubletree Dr. |
| Highland Village, Texas 75077 |
| Toll Free (866) 229-2665 |
| (972) 317-6404 Fax |

Name _____

Address_____

City_____State_____Zip_____

Telephone (Day)_____(Evening)_____

— —

To Order: *To order Easy Desserts*

Please send_____ hardcover copies @ $19.95 (U.S.) each $ _____

Texas residents add sales tax @ $1.60 each $ _____

Please send_____ paperback copies @ $16.95 (U.S.) each $_____

Texas residents add sales tax @ $1.34 each $_____

Plus postage/handling @ $6.00 (1st copy) $ _____

$1.00 (each additional copy) $ _____

Check or Credit Card (Canada-credit card only) **Total** $ _____

Charge to: ❑ MasterCard.   or   ❑ VISA

Account # _____

Expiration Date _____

Signature_____

| Mail or Call: |
| Cookbook Resources |
| 541 Doubletree Dr. |
| Highland Village, Texas 75077 |
| Toll Free (866) 229-2665 |
| (972) 317-6404 Fax |

Name _____

Address_____

City_____State_____Zip_____

Telephone (Day)_____(Evening)_____